OPPOSING
VIEWPOINTS®
SERIES

W9-BUB-842

Sexually
Transmitted Diseases

Other Books of Related Interest:

Opposing Viewpoints Series

Domestic Violence

Health Care

Online Pornography

Street Teens

Teenage Sexuality

At Issue Series

Alcohol Abuse

Cyberpredators

Gay Marriage

Health Care Legislation

Current Controversies Series

Gays in the Military

The Uninsured

Vaccines

"Congress shall make
no law . . . abridging
the freedom of speech,
or of the press."

First Amendment to the US Constitution

The basic foundation of our democracy is the First Amendment guarantee of freedom of expression. The *Opposing Viewpoints* series is dedicated to the concept of this basic freedom
and the idea that it is more important to practice it than to en-
shrine it.

OPPOSING VIEWPOINTS® SERIES

Sexually Transmitted Diseases

Roman Espejo, Book Editor

GREENHAVEN PRESS
A part of Gale, Cengage Learning

Detroit • New York • San Francisco • New Haven, Conn • Waterville, Maine • London

Christine Nasso, *Publisher*
Elizabeth Des Chenes, *Managing Editor*

© 2011 Greenhaven Press, a part of Gale, Cengage Learning

Gale and Greenhaven Press are registered trademarks used herein under license.

For more information, contact:
Greenhaven Press
27500 Drake Rd.
Farmington Hills, MI 48331-3535
Or you can visit our Internet site at gale.cengage.com

For product information and technology assistance, contact us at

Gale Customer Support, 1-800-877-4253
For permission to use material from this text or product, submit all requests online at
www.cengage.com/permissions

Further permissions questions can be emailed to permissionrequest@cengage.com

Articles in Greenhaven Press anthologies are often edited for length to meet page requirements. In addition, original titles of these works are changed to clearly present the main thesis and to explicitly indicate the author's opinion. Every effort is made to ensure that Greenhaven Press accurately reflects the original intent of the authors. Every effort has been made to trace the owners of copyrighted material.

Cover image copyright © photos.com/Getty Images.

LIBRARY OF CONGRESS CATALOGING-IN-PUBLICATION DATA

Sexually transmitted diseases / Roman Espejo, book editor.
   p. cm. -- (Opposing viewpoints)
  Includes bibliographical references and index.
  ISBN 978-0-7377-5237-3 (hardcover) -- ISBN 978-0-7377-5238-0 (pbk.)
  1. Sexually transmitted diseases. I. Espejo, Roman, 1977-
  RA644.V4.S36795 2011
  362.196'951--dc22

               2010043633

Printed in the United States of America
2 3 4 5 6   15 14 13 12 11

FD189

Contents

Chapter 3: How Can the Spread of Sexually Transmitted Diseases Be Reduced?

Chapter 4: How Should the Global AIDS Crisis Be Addressed?

Why Consider Opposing Viewpoints?

> *"The only way in which a human being can make some approach to knowing the whole of a subject is by hearing what can be said about it by persons of every variety of opinion and studying all modes in which it can be looked at by every character of mind. No wise man ever acquired his wisdom in any mode but this."*
>
> *John Stuart Mill*

In our media-intensive culture it is not difficult to find differing opinions. Thousands of newspapers and magazines and dozens of radio and television talk shows resound with differing points of view. The difficulty lies in deciding which opinion to agree with and which "experts" seem the most credible. The more inundated we become with differing opinions and claims, the more essential it is to hone critical reading and thinking skills to evaluate these ideas. Opposing Viewpoints books address this problem directly by presenting stimulating debates that can be used to enhance and teach these skills. The varied opinions contained in each book examine many different aspects of a single issue. While examining these conveniently edited opposing views, readers can develop critical thinking skills such as the ability to compare and contrast authors' credibility, facts, argumentation styles, use of persuasive techniques, and other stylistic tools. In short, the Opposing Viewpoints Series is an ideal way to attain the higher-level thinking and reading skills so essential in a culture of diverse and contradictory opinions.

In addition to providing a tool for critical thinking, *Opposing Viewpoints* books challenge readers to question their own strongly held opinions and assumptions. Most people form their opinions on the basis of upbringing, peer pressure, and personal, cultural, or professional bias. By reading carefully balanced opposing views, readers must directly confront new ideas as well as the opinions of those with whom they disagree. This is not to argue simplistically that everyone who reads opposing views will—or should—change his or her opinion. Instead, the series enhances readers' understanding of their own views by encouraging confrontation with opposing ideas. Careful examination of others' views can lead to the readers' understanding of the logical inconsistencies in their own opinions, perspective on why they hold an opinion, and the consideration of the possibility that their opinion requires further evaluation.

Evaluating Other Opinions

To ensure that this type of examination occurs, *Opposing Viewpoints* books present all types of opinions. Prominent spokespeople on different sides of each issue as well as well-known professionals from many disciplines challenge the reader. An additional goal of the series is to provide a forum for other, less known, or even unpopular viewpoints. The opinion of an ordinary person who has had to make the decision to cut off life support from a terminally ill relative, for example, may be just as valuable and provide just as much insight as a medical ethicist's professional opinion. The editors have two additional purposes in including these less known views. One, the editors encourage readers to respect others' opinions—even when not enhanced by professional credibility. It is only by reading or listening to and objectively evaluating others' ideas that one can determine whether they are worthy of consideration. Two, the inclusion of such viewpoints encourages the important critical thinking skill of objectively evaluating an author's credentials and bias. This evaluation will illuminate an author's reasons for taking a particular stance on an issue and will aid in readers' evaluation of the author's ideas.

It is our hope that these books will give readers a deeper understanding of the issues debated and an appreciation of the complexity of even seemingly simple issues when good and honest people disagree. This awareness is particularly important in a democratic society such as ours in which people enter into public debate to determine the common good. Those with whom one disagrees should not be regarded as enemies but rather as people whose views deserve careful examination and may shed light on one's own.

Thomas Jefferson once said that "difference of opinion leads to inquiry, and inquiry to truth." Jefferson, a broadly educated man, argued that "if a nation expects to be ignorant and free . . . it expects what never was and never will be." As individuals and as a nation, it is imperative that we consider the opinions of others and examine them with skill and discernment. The *Opposing Viewpoints* series is intended to help readers achieve this goal.

David L. Bender and Bruno Leone,
Founders

Introduction

The most common sexually transmitted disease (STD) is the human papillomavirus (HPV), which can cause fleshy growths on the genitals or anus. More than thirty types have been identified, and about 20 million Americans have HPV. In fact, at least 50 percent of adults are infected during their lifetime—most asymptomatic and some carrying several types at once—with 1 percent showing symptoms at any time. If they appear (from several weeks to years after infection), genital warts, which can be caused by HPV, may go away on their own or remain the same. But severe or persistent cases may require procedures such as cryosurgery or laser treatment. Some people deal with outbreaks for years, as treatment does not eradicate the virus.

While the immune system clears HPV within two years in 90 percent of individuals, high-risk types trigger virtually all cases of cervical cancer and are linked to vulvar, vaginal, penile, and anal cancer. In 2008, eleven thousand newly reported infections of cervical cancer with 3,900 deaths occurred in the United States. According to the World Health Organization, cervical cancer ranks fifth as the deadliest cancer for women; HPV causes cervical dysplasia, the painful growth of precancerous cells, affecting up to 1 million American women a year.

HPV is detected in women with a Pap smear, wherein cells are scraped from the cervix and examined under a microscope for abnormal cells. Two strains—types 16 and 18—are believed to cause 70 percent of all cervical cancer cases. (Types 6 and 11 cause 90 percent of all genital warts cases.) Wearing a condom during intercourse can also cut the risk of HPV, but it only partially covers the genital area during intercourse.

The introduction of Gardasil in 2006—an immunization against types 6, 11, 16, and 18—is regarded as a major advancement against HPV and cervical cancer. "Widespread vaccination has the potential to reduce cervical cancer deaths around the world by as much as two-thirds, if all women were to take the vaccine and if protection turns out to be long-term,"[1] asserts the National Cancer Institute. "In addition, the vaccines can reduce the need for medical care, biopsies, and invasive procedures associated with the follow-up from abnormal Pap tests, thus helping to reduce health care costs and anxieties related to abnormal Pap tests and follow-up procedures." The Food and Drug Administration (FDA) approved Gardasil for females and males from nine to twenty-six years of age. Research purports it to be nearly 100 percent effective for four years. (Its efficacy over a lifetime and need for a booster shot is still being studied.) Kari Lange, an Illinois mother, had her two teenage daughters inoculated with the HPV vaccine. "To me it wasn't even about sex,"[2] explains Lange. "It was just healthy for the kids."

1. "National Cancer Institute Factsheet: Human Papillomavirus (HPV) Vaccines," August 2010. www.cancer.gov.
2. Karen Springen, "Why Are HPV Vaccine Rates So Low?" *Newsweek*, February 24, 2008. www.newsweek.com.

Nonetheless, it is about the sex to some parents who declined Gardasil for their children. "We haven't even talked about the birds and the bees yet,"[3] asserts Amy Groff, a mother in Ohio, who did not seek the vaccine for her daughter at age eleven. "She needs to be innocent a little bit longer." Her opinion reflects the deeper concern that Gardasil may influence the early initiation of sexual activity. Much more urgent, however, are the allegations that Gardasil leads to adverse reactions and illnesses in young women—including the muscle disorder Guillain-Barré syndrome, joint pain, and migraines. "There is no known treatment to help these girls as they suffer in silence. The doctors, if they even admit the connection, have no idea how to help them,"[4] reads a statement from the Truth About Gardasil website. Moreover, as of May 2010, fifty-three females in the United States died after receiving the vaccine, twenty-nine of which have been confirmed. A federal report named complications such as foaming at the mouth, anaphylactic shock, and coma. "Gardasil vaccine was inappropriately fast tracked and licensed by the FDA and recommended by the CDC [Centers for Disease Control and Prevention] with too little attention paid to the reports of brain and immune system dysfunction that developed after vaccination in pre-licensure clinical trials,"[5] argues Barbara Loe Fisher, cofounder and president of the National Vaccine Information Center. "That same cavalier attitude toward Gardasil-related deaths and serious health problems, which have been experienced by many girls and young women after licensure, is inexcusable."

Gardasil is one of the preventative measures against STDs, none of which—from condoms to virginity pledges—has es-

3. Rob Stein, "Vaccine for Girls Raises Thorny Issues," *Washington Post*, November 7, 2006. www.washingtonpost.com.
4. "The Truth About Gardasil," Truthaboutgardasil.org, August 27, 2010. http://truthaboutgardasil.org.
5. Barbara Loe Fisher, "Gardasil Death & Brain Damage: A National Tragedy," *Vaccine Awakening* (blog), February 9, 2009. http://vaccineawakening.blogspot.com.

caped controversy. *Opposing Viewpoints: Sexually Transmitted Diseases* delves into the issue of STD prevention and more in the following chapters: Are Sexually Transmitted Diseases a Serious Problem? How Should Students Be Educated About Sexually Transmitted Diseases? How Can the Spread of Sexually Transmitted Diseases Be Reduced? and How Should the Global AIDS Crisis Be Addressed? The authors of the viewpoints in this book confront these challenges and address the physical, public, and personal impact of STDs.

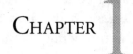

CHAPTER 1

Are Sexually Transmitted Diseases a Serious Problem?

Chapter Preface

Reported cases of chlamydia hit a record 1.2 million in 2008, leaping from 1.1 million in 2007. Adolescent girls from fifteen to nineteen years old had the highest rate at 3,276 cases per 100,000. Young women from twenty to twenty-four years old followed closely at 3,180 cases per 100,000. "This likely reflects a combination of factors, including biological differences that place females at greater risk for STDs [sexually transmitted diseases] than males, as well as higher STD screening rates among young women," states the Centers for Disease Control and Prevention (CDC). Females have rates that are three times higher than males.

Philadelphia, Pennsylvania, is hard hit by chlamydia. Between 2007 and 2008, 721 of the 15,090 students screened for the disease tested positive. "Everybody in the 'hood burnin'," [1] says a teen who identified himself as "Bubba," who picked up free condoms. "People try to hide it, but people know." In fact, 10 percent of female residents from fifteen to nineteen years old reported being infected in 2009, the same year that Philadelphia ranked third for such cases. "Once a disease gets introduced into a population, it can be very difficult to break the cycle of infection," [2] claims Melinda Salmon who is program manager at the city's STD Control Program. Overall, Philadelphians are more than five times as likely to have chlamydia than other state residents.

A bacterial infection, chlamydia is called a "silent" disease because up to 75 percent of individuals infected do not show symptoms, which include penile or vaginal discharge, pain or burning sensation during urination for males, and pelvic pain for women. It is easily tested and treated, but when it goes un-

---

1. Natalie Pompilio, "A City on Fire: Explosive Rise in Number of Young Adults with STDs," *Philadelphia Daily News*, August 20, 2010. www.philly.com.
2. Ibid.

detected, it can result in pelvic inflammatory disease among women, in which scarring in the fallopian tubes may form and cause infertility. In the following chapter, the authors frame the discussion and debate of STDs in the context of public health.

| *"But in fact sexually transmitted diseases are so common that they're a problem for everyone."*

STDs Are a Serious Problem

Lisa Kaiser

In the following viewpoint, Lisa Kaiser claims that sexually transmitted diseases (STDs) threaten public health at a national level, reinforced by the startling rates among poor minority youths in Milwaukee, Wisconsin. Kaiser maintains that the problem is exacerbated by several factors in this population including the realization that low-income adolescents are less likely to buy condoms and are more prone to engage in high-risk behaviors. Moreover, she insists that sex education programs in Milwaukee schools are inconsistent, with some offering none or little real-world knowledge to students. The author is the news editor for the website ExpressMilwaukee.com.

As you read, consider the following questions:

1. What statistics does Kaiser provide to illustrate the STD problem in Milwaukee?

2. What is Kaiser's view of abstinence-only education?

Lisa Kaiser, "The Silent Epidemic," ExpressMilwaukee.com, May 21, 2008. Reproduced by permission.

3. In Geoffrey Swain's opinion, why are low-income groups more likely to engage in at-risk behaviors?

Many were shocked when the Centers for Disease Control and Prevention (CDC) reported last year [2007] that one in four teenage girls had contracted a sexually transmitted disease (STD). But Milwaukee experts weren't. Milwaukee has a long-standing problem not only with teen pregnancy, but with teen STDs as well.

The city routinely rates in the top five or 10 cities for chlamydia, gonorrhea and teen pregnancy. Milwaukee County accounts for 50% of all STDs in the state of Wisconsin, and the city of Milwaukee has the 10th highest rate of STD infection among the 63 cities studied by the CDC.

The rate of infection is hitting the city's minority and teen residents especially hard. African Americans account for 49% of all reported STDs in the city. In the neighborhoods with the highest rate of STDs, 22% of 15–19-year-olds had an STD.

"I would say that the Milwaukee community has done a poor job of ensuring that teenagers and sexually active young adults know about their risks and how to prevent those risks, as well as having the resources to prevent those risks," said former Milwaukee health commissioner Seth Foldy, M.D., who now heads up the Milwaukee Alliance for Sexual Health (MASH).

Milwaukee's Alarmingly High Rates of Teens with STDs

MASH, a project funded by the Healthier Wisconsin Partnership Program of the Medical College of Wisconsin, is bringing together community organizations and medical professionals to look into why so many Milwaukee teens—especially African American teens—become pregnant or infected with STDs, and what can be done about it.

It's not surprising that the two problems are intertwined, since unprotected sex leads to both unintended pregnancies and STDs. "I don't think we can address teen pregnancy without addressing sexually transmitted diseases, and we can't address sexually transmitted diseases without addressing pregnancy," said Geoffrey Swain, M.D., associate medical director of the city of Milwaukee Public Health Department and an associate professor of family medicine [at] UW[University of Wisconsin]-Madison School of Medicine and Public Health.

But unlike the highly visible epidemic of teen pregnancy, teens with STDs aren't as easy to identify. In fact, many have no symptoms, so many infected teens aren't tested or treated. Untreated STDs have serious health consequences, such [as] infertility, pelvic inflammatory disease, tubal pregnancies [and] cervical cancer.

"These are not minor issues," Swain said. "These are very serious, life-changing issues. Everyone knows that teen pregnancy is a life-changing issue, but people don't necessarily see that sexually transmitted diseases are, too."

Why Is It So Bad?

Point to inconsistent messages about sexual responsibility, poverty and lack of hope in the future as reasons why Milwaukee has such high rates of teen STDs. Certainly, all experts are quick to endorse abstinence as the best safeguard against becoming pregnant or contracting an STD.

Foldy said teaching about abstinence, as promoted by conservatives, is important for teens who don't want [to] become sexually active. But abstinence-only education doesn't necessarily lead to a reduction in the number of [those] who have sex; in fact, students who receive comprehensive sex education are more likely to delay having sex and use contraceptives.

"Abstinence education is important, but not enough," Foldy said.

The Milwaukee Public Schools (MPS) system has a well-thought-out comprehensive human development curriculum, Foldy said, that includes not only information about STDs and pregnancy, but has skill-building activities as well, so students can implement that knowledge in the real world.

"But that curriculum is not delivered uniformly," Foldy said. "Many schools offer none of it. Some schools offer a tiny amount of it. It is up to the school to decide how it will be offered or whether it's going to be offered."

Lacking this universal implementation, MPS schools can invite outside educators . . . for their students. (MPS did not return a request to comment for this [viewpoint].)

Adding to this lack of a consistent message about safe sexual practices is the high level of poverty in Milwaukee. Swain said that Milwaukee's unusually high rates of poverty—especially child poverty—contribute to the STD epidemic, not only because low-income teens aren't likely to spend money on condoms, but because they aren't connecting safe sex practices to their future well-being.

"A group of people who are very poor, struggling to get by, don't see a lot of hope for the future, and they're less likely to act now in a way that will protect them in the future," Swain said. Swain said that while people with STDs are more likely to be found in the poorer, predominantly African American neighborhoods in Milwaukee, the behaviors that lead to unintended pregnancy and STDs can be found everywhere.

"At an individual level, what it boils down to is how many partners have you had, do you use condoms and do you engage in behaviors that impair your judgment, such as using drugs or alcohol while having sex, or trading drugs for sex," Swain said. "Many affluent white teenagers have the same behaviors, and certainly older adults who are affluent and white have multiple partners. There are fewer of them, statistically speaking, but those individuals are at very high risk for sexually transmitted diseases."

To help ensure that teens have access to condoms, a good way to prevent most STDs and pregnancy, the city of Milwaukee—with help from volunteers, outside donors and fundraising efforts, such as the AIDS Walk—launched the "No Condom, No Way" campaign, which distributes free condoms and information about safe sex in friendly places. "It was important for us to combine the condom with the message," Foldy said.

What Can Be Done?

Blaming teens for being less-than-completely responsible isn't going to solve the city's STD and unintended pregnancy problems. So MASH is currently studying successful safe sex programs in other cities and states with the hopes of replicating them in Milwaukee.

Foldy said that some good policies—such as New York's distribution of condoms in public schools—wouldn't fly in Milwaukee, even though they could help reduce the number of unintended pregnancies and STDs among city youths.

More resources for the city's health department workers who track down partners of those who have been infected with an STD would also help, Foldy said. "We are reaching a small proportion of these contacts," Foldy said.

He added that other states allow doctors to provide prescriptions not only for their patient who has tested positive for an STD, but for their partner as well. A recent effort to make this legal in Wisconsin died in the state legislature. "It won't be perfect, but you will eliminate a huge number of barriers," Foldy said.

Foldy added that MASH is hoping to improve care at clinic level, by increasing patients' enrollment in the Family Planning Waiver Program or BadgerCare, and urging primary care physicians to routinely screen patients for STDs. Alternate sites for testing—such as schools or community organizations—could also be explored.

Foldy said raising awareness of the impact of STDs on [the] public's health and the city's future is important at every level, from an individual's health to the cost of treatment of cancer and infertility in the decades to come.

"I think people tend to say this is a problem for [some] people, but not for everyone," Foldy said. "But in fact sexually transmitted diseases are so common that they're a problem for everyone."

"[Not engaging in 'normal' sexual activity is] an acute response to the culture of condoms and caution, a sexual dysfunction that's grown out of the safe-sex campaign."

Fears of STDs Are Exaggerated

Grant Stoddard

Grant Stoddard is a writer based in British Columbia, Canada, and is the author of Working Stiff: The Misadventures of an Accidental Sexpert. *In the following viewpoint, Stoddard contends that more single heterosexual adults in their twenties and thirties are overly cautious of sexually transmitted diseases (STDs) and take drastic measures to protect themselves or completely abstain from sexual activity. The revelation that condoms are not totally effective against herpes and genital warts, he claims, lead many individuals to avoid sexual contact or misdiagnose themselves. With fears blown out of proportion, many deny themselves of one of life's greatest human pleasures and most basic fulfillments, Stoddard concludes.*

As you read, consider the following questions:

1. What figures does Stoddard cite for the rates of herpes and genital warts?

Grant Stoddard, "Sex/steria," *New York Magazine*, May 21, 2005. Reproduced by permission.

2. How does the Internet worsen anxieties of having an STD, as described by the author?

3. How does Stoddard support his claim that worries about STDs among the public do not reflect the reality?

Twenty-four-year-old Lindsey is attractive, vivacious, flirtatious, and perennially single. She loves men and says that she really enjoys sex. Her stylishly shaggy hair looks freshly tugged, but despite appearances, Lindsey hasn't gotten past second base in the past twelve months. Her fear of catching a sexually transmitted disease is so acute that she's taking the only measure she believes will put her chances of contracting an STD closer to zero.

"When I was 20, I gave this one guy I liked a blow job—just once, and my pants stayed on," explains Lindsey (all those who spoke about their sex lives for this [viewpoint] are identified by middle name). "A month later, I got a little red bump [*points, whispers*] down there, and based on what I'd read on the Internet, became convinced that he'd given me herpes." Devastated and embarrassed, she began comparing the bump with pictorial examples on the web. Confronted with the mass of statistical data on communicable conditions, she crunched numbers and tried to reconcile them with the 72-hour false prophet in her underpants—which eventually transpired to be nothing more than an ingrown hair. "I hardly slept a wink, and the percentages just kept whizzing around in my head. What I learned about STDs and how thinking I had herpes made me feel, well," she pauses to self-medicate with a sip of her margarita, "I never, ever want to feel that way again."

Having sex with a rotating cast of interesting characters is what twentysomething New Yorkers do. It's practically in the job description. Yet Lindsey is one of a small but growing number of young, single, heterosexual Manhattanites so utterly spooked by the prospect of catching a sexually transmitted disease that engaging in "normal" sexual activity has simply become an unjustifiable risk. It's an acute response to the culture of condoms and caution, a sexual dysfunction that's grown out of the safe-sex campaign.

Anyone who came of age in the past twenty years can't be blamed for equating sex with undesirable consequences. The AIDS [acquired immune deficiency syndrome] epidemic was in full swing before this generation even started thinking about having sex. [Singer-songwriter] Freddie Mercury died, [basketball player] Magic Johnson announced he was HIV-positive, and an unusually grave Madonna laid out the case for condoms from a gritty high school set in a public service announcement. Then there were the warnings closer to home.

Anne, a 28-year-old writer who won't have sexual contact with anyone unless he first submits to the full range of STD tests, says her stringency comes from her school's self-preservation programs in the late eighties. "When my sixth-grade health teacher told us that smoking causes lung cancer, I decided right then that I would never put a cigarette to my lips," she says. "When my seventh-grade health teacher told us that dropping LSD would cause us to hurl ourselves out of fifth-story windows believing we could fly, I vowed never to take acid as long as I lived. And when my eighth-grade health teacher told us about the horrors of HIV [human immunodeficiency virus], I took extensive notes."

The purpose of sex education was not to prevent people like Anne from having satisfying sex lives when they grew up; it was to encourage them to be "safe." Condoms were the literal catchalls that facilitated business as usual in the eighties and nineties. But with recent data suggesting that condoms may not protect against the transmission of all STDs, safe sex has been rebranded with a disconcerting title: "safer" sex. No guarantees.

The rug pulled out from under them, single New Yorkers are reevaluating the risk-versus-reward of sex. For most people, this simply means more carefully considering the consequences of their actions; for Anne, it means no action. She rarely has sex at all these days—her strict requirements don't allow for casual encounters, even with condoms. "I do wish every once in a while that I had the personality where I could just f--- whomever I wanted to at random and at whim," she says. "But I never really bought into the whole idea—that some of my well-educated, worldly, sophisticated peers hold dear—that people like us don't get sick."

The new age of "safer" sex has its own sexual bogeymen: herpes and the human papillomavirus (HPV). Though they're not life-threatening, these two diseases are transmitted by skin-to-skin contact, which makes them loom larger in the imagination than even HIV. And it doesn't take much imagination to see every potential partner as a potential health hazard. Between a fifth and a quarter of all Americans have genital herpes, and the majority of Americans are carriers of the strain that causes cold sores, which can be transmitted to the genitals. HPV, the virus that causes genital warts and can lead to cervical cancer if left untreated, is even more common: Up to 75 percent of the reproductive-age population is infected. And as with herpes, those who have HPV might not ever know it. That's a lot of secret Santas out there.

To make matters more frightening, most young people get their STD information from the Internet, where no more or less weight is given to a site produced by the Centers for Disease Control [and Prevention], an abstinence group, a drug company hawking a product, or a lowly blogger spinning a yarn about how he contracted pubic lice from his cousin's dachshund. "It can be a double-edged sword, this information age," says Evelyn Intondi, a nurse-midwife at Planned Parenthood of New York City. "If you are compulsively consulting websites for this stuff, you can pretty quickly work yourself up. I mean, you can Google something, and there are thousands of websites on this subject. Finding out about STDs in this way can be very scary."

Finding out about *any* illness this way can be scary. Go online for information about moles, and it's not hard to convince yourself you've got skin cancer. Out of breath after a workout? You can quickly match up your symptoms with adult-onset asthma. Feeling clumsy and uncoordinated? Better get checked for MS [multiple sclerosis]. The Internet is like oxygen to a hypochondriac's fire, turning general anxiety into a full-blown, life-altering obsession. "People pick up fragmented information," explains Zachary Bregman, an internist and assistant clinical professor at the Albert Einstein College of Medicine. "There is an increasing degree of hypochondria among young people in general. If it was something I saw in 2 or 3 percent of people before, I'm seeing it in 6 percent now." And most of the hypochondriacs, says Bregman, are fixated on STDs—diseases so personal and stigmatized that they lend themselves to private, panicky surf sessions. The millions of sexual health sites, with their warnings and statistics and symptoms, are daunting even in a sober state of mind. But after a night of intoxicated sex and a burning sensation upon urination, a web search can lead to an unqualified diagnosis, paranoia, and a sharp shift—temporary or permanent—in sexual behavior.

A Social Disease

James, a 30-year-old PR [public relations] account exec, isn't taking any chances. Though he's not abstaining from sex, James does all he can to decrease his risk while he plays the field. His precautions have become the stuff of legend among those who have been invited up to his Murray Hill duplex. "I always wear a condom, even during foreplay," he says with evangelical zeal. "And I use plastic wrap as an oral dam when giving head. I've had some who really don't like it at all, but most say it was 90 percent as good." James also won't receive oral sex without barrier protection; he puts on a condom and then adjourns to the shower to wash off the taste. "A lot of women don't like condoms," he says. "Tough. Neither do I. However, the next morning, I can feel relaxed and can go about my life. . . . Two hours of enjoyment never outweighs weeks of worry, trips to the doctor, and potentially lifelong issues."

Like Lindsey, James's STD obsession has led him to mistake a common malady for a social disease. When he was 23, he became convinced that his first bladder infection was really the result of a night when he was not quite so vigilant. He submitted to a battery of STD tests, some of them painful. "Ever since then," he says, "if a girl will go down on me without a condom, say, on a first date, I know that in all likelihood she did that with someone else the night before."

Not content to worry only about STDs, James makes a habit of using three, preferably four, methods of contraception simultaneously. "I'll use a condom, she'll be on the Pill, and I'll pull out, too. Of course, getting someone pregnant would be a nightmare. The condom box claims a 98 percent rate of effectiveness; when I pull out, I take care of the other 2 percent."

Sex is a numbers game for safe-sex obsessives, but in terms of numbers, the obsession may be spreading even faster than the diseases. Calls to the CDC's national STD and AIDS hotline rose from about 650,000 in 2001 to 777,266 in 2003—an increase of over 19 percent. Catherine Wild, a health-communication specialist who has been answering hotline queries for the past six years, says that herpes and HPV calls are the ones coming in fast and furious—this despite an overall 17 percent *decrease* in the rate of genital herpes infection since the early nineties.

"In light of people realizing that condoms aren't totally effective at preventing the transmission of herpes and HPV because the condom doesn't cover the whole genital area, we get people asking how much of their body they should cover in Saran Wrap," Wild says. "People also test obsessively. They may have been at risk for something two years ago, but still test every month, even if they haven't had a partner since. Obviously they come up negative. It's an anxiety disorder. We can't help beyond explaining the process. We suggest they consider seeing a mental health professional."

Robert Salant, a clinical associate professor of urology at NYU [New York University] Medical Center and a physician at Midtown Urologic Associates, has seen these obsessives in his practice. He notes a 35 percent increase in self-referred patients in the past two years: "More and more frequently, my patients come in for evaluation for a potential STD armed with pages of Internet articles or already 'self-diagnosed.' Sometimes they are right, and sometimes they are wrong."

While Salant suggests that the advantages of increased public awareness outweigh the disadvantages of unfiltered information, he has witnessed the consequences of Internet-spawned STD paranoia. "I have definitely had the occasion when a patient came to me convinced he had HPV, yet there was absolutely no objective evidence of infection," he says. "One young man had seen six physicians prior to visiting with me. He was upset that the previous six had missed the HPV diagnosis. He was even more upset when I examined him and found no evidence of disease. I often wonder how many more doctors he visited before he finally believed he was fine."

In Dr. Bregman's experience, this kind of STD paranoia is an almost exclusively heterosexual phenomenon. He rarely sees it in his gay patients, despite the fact that HIV infection is again on the rise in that community. His straight patients, however, particularly the men, mirror those of Dr. Salant's. "There is an increase in patient requests for STD testing to a level that is not always medically justified," he says. "And some continue to believe they have a disease when good testing—accurate 99 out of a hundred times—tells them they don't."

While these doctors understand their patients' STD concerns, they don't think their fear is warranted. "There is some research suggesting that the herpes virus may not be completely contained by the use of condoms," admits Salant. "But a larger body of literature suggests that latex condoms do indeed prevent the transmission. I rarely, if ever, recommend abstinence as a primary method to combat the spread of STDs."

Starving Themselves Sexually

Most safe-sex obsessives take extreme measures because they are afraid of catching an STD, but 32-year-old Richard has given up sex because he is afraid of spreading one. Eighteen months ago, he was diagnosed with genital warts. "It was maddening," Richard explains. "I'd have the warts lasered off, and because of the scars the procedure leaves, I was out of commission for weeks on end." The doctor told him that after three wart-free months, he could safely dive back into the dating pool—with condoms, of course. But soon after starting a new relationship, the warts would return. HPV outbreaks have been linked to stress, and Richard was under plenty of it. "I'd get overcome with the guilt and shame of not telling them about my past health issues that I thought were history," he says. "I'd just have to make up an excuse and end the relationship and then start the cycle all over again."

After leaving four confused girls in his wake, Richard decided abstinence would be simpler, and safer. "The problem is not going without sex but explaining not taking girls home. It's actually aphrodisiacal when you are sexually aloof with an attractive girl, but a couple of them have spread rumors about me being gay. I think this might be a good time to join the Peace Corps."

According to sex therapist Jean Moné, Richard's decision is not all that unusual. "People are starving themselves sexually and sometimes need an excuse to do that. Germs and disease can provide that excuse," she explains. "It's a sexual anorexia. People can go into this high-risk Orange Alert mind-set of 'I don't want to take risks; I don't want to have sex at all.' Being intimate is when we take off the mask and show our true selves to the other person, warts and all." Moné's use of the phrase is deliberate. "Warts can be burned off. Other stuff you can take antibiotics for. With herpes, most people only get a few outbreaks a year. If you can be responsible with it, well, there are a lot worse things."

This kind of rationalization is no comfort to safe-sex obsessives. "Try explaining you only have a few outbreaks a year to an attractive female who doesn't have herpes," says James, his face turning red. "Second date? I think not. Even if she accepted it, long-term sex would always need to be with a condom. Even with daily medication, it's a fact that it can still spread at the beginning of an outbreak without visible symptoms."

James's diligent use of condoms and plastic wrap is one thing, but isn't abstaining entirely a disproportionate reaction to the risk? Isn't it unhealthy to forgo one of life's most basic needs and greatest pleasures in pursuit of health? At the suggestion that giving up sex for fear of disease was like giving up eating for fear of food poisoning, Lindsey's expression sours. She is unconvinced. "There's no shame in getting food poisoning from sushi, but goddamned genital warts? I mean, how do I tell my mom about that?"

> *"Many older gay men now believe that some younger ones are blasé, even reckless about contracting HIV."*

HIV Is a Serious Problem for Gay Men

Carol Midgley

In the following viewpoint, Carol Midgley argues that today's generation of homosexual men has become complacent about HIV and the ravages of AIDS, engaging in unsafe sex practices. Medical breakthroughs in managing the virus and the longtime survival of many HIV-positive individuals have shaped changing attitudes toward safe sex, she claims. In England, however, the populations with HIV are growing, the author continues, and a renewed public campaign against HIV and AIDS targeted toward young gay men is necessary. Midgley is a writer and columnist for the Times, *a daily national newspaper in the United Kingdom.*

As you read, consider the following questions:

1. How does the author support her claim that HIV is on the rise in England?

Carol Midgley, "HIV and the Rise of Complacency," *Times Online*, June 15, 2010. Reproduced by permission.

2. According to Karl Riley, what aspects of contemporary gay culture contribute to lax attitudes toward safe sex?

3. What social cost would occur with the return of an HIV epidemic, as stated by Midgley?

There's a scene in Jonathan Harvey's play, *Canary*, in which two gay men—one young, one middle-aged—are about to have sex with each other for the first time. The younger one announces that he is into "BB"—barebacked sex or sex without a condom. His older conquest is appalled. "What if I'm HIV?" he demands. The younger man shrugs. "So what if you do give me something?" he replies. "I'll just take pills."

Of all the scenes in Harvey's acclaimed drama about homosexual experience over the past five decades this one is attracting the most attention. This is because it epitomises an issue worrying many people within the gay community—a new complacency about HIV [human immunodeficiency virus].

Many older gay men now believe that some younger ones are blasé, even reckless about contracting HIV. There's a significant minority, they believe, who regards it as no more serious than any other sexually transmitted disease, comforted by the availability of powerful antiretroviral drugs and the message that it's now a "manageable illness".

There are even claims of some men knowingly exposing themselves to the virus thinking it "no big deal". Critics say that health campaigners have been so concerned to destigmatise HIV that they have softened its image.

Harvey, 42, noticed the shift about five years ago, and believes that it coincided with HIV-infected people surviving for many years on combination therapy. He says that he is aware of "younger people who see unsafe sex as an option, a risk worth taking, and more enjoyable and exciting". They "see an interest in safe sex as boring and fuddy-duddy and old-fashioned". As the young man, Toby, says in Harvey's play "HIV's like an old man's disease. It's so last century".

Beneath the Radar

Of course, those under 23 weren't even born when the grim tombstone public health adverts blitzed our TV screens in 1987. Most of today's young gay men have never attended the funeral of someone who has perished from AIDS [acquired immune deficiency syndrome]. They probably cannot imagine just how much stigma there was. Life has moved on and for the straight community too. HIV has dipped beneath the radar. We vaguely assume it's a virus that has been conquered. It hasn't.

Within the past decade the infection rate in this country has doubled. Statistics from the Terrence Higgins Trust show that in 2008 there were more than 7,000 new diagnoses. Ten years earlier in 1998 there were fewer than 3,000. Of those new diagnoses in 2008, 38 per cent were among men who have sex with men. Roughly two-thirds of the total of infected people were male. The largest proportion of the heterosexual group is black Africans, many of whom would have caught HIV in Africa but have received the diagnosis in the UK [United Kingdom]. In 2008, 571 people died from HIV-related illness.

Many gay men believe that tougher campaigns are needed. Karl Riley, 24, a journalist who writes about gay issues says this is a "confused generation" receiving conflicting messages. Recent health campaigns have focused on how to "minimise the risks" rather than vetoing unprotected sex. Meanwhile, a culture is flourishing, fuelled by gay pornography, glamorising "barebacking", perpetuating the message that "only unsafe sex is real sex". Riley says: "Our generation has not lost people to this disease. We've had a very different experience of HIV ... but we need to be told the top line. We need to know how many people are getting it and to have a better awareness of what HIV can do."

It was Riley who broke the story about three young men who contracted HIV on the British set of a porn film, shot without condoms. One of them, interviewed for *Boyz* magazine and *Newsnight* said that he "wasn't bothered he had HIV, and that being gay he always knew he'd get it". In a debate on the issue, *Time Out*'s Paul Burston told of a conversation he'd had with a 22-year-old in Liverpool, who said he was more worried about catching gonorrhea [a sexually transmitted disease] than HIV. As Riley says of his generation: "We're not scared of HIV, and it's no wonder. Sex education in schools barely touches on HIV and gay sex. . . . HIV prevention charities [should] catch those who fall through the net. Yet instead of giving us a picture of what our lives could be like if we bareback, they choose to empower us."

This new insouciance is also giving rise to wild claims, such as that some actively seek out the virus wanting to belong to its "community". A subculture known as "bug-chasing" in which individuals pursue sex with HIV-infected people has its own Wikipedia entry though most experts say there is no evidence to support it and it's largely a myth.

Harvey, who wrote *Beautiful Thing*, the BBC sitcom *Gimme Gimme Gimme* and is a scriptwriter for *Coronation Street*, says one of the things which motivated him to write *Canary* was that, because most gay men don't have children, important stories weren't being passed down the generations. "I know all about my family from my grandma but if you don't have kids who do those stories get passed on to?" he asks. "I've lived all my sexually active life knowing about HIV and AIDS. There wasn't a time when I didn't know you had to wear a condom . . . it's different for this generation. But the show isn't just about this. It's about a bigger apathy. In my day we had [British prime minister Margaret] Thatcher and one of the benefits of that was that she made such horrible laws about gay people we all clubbed together and made a stand. It kept the community together. That's lacking now. There's not really a common cause to fight against."

A Very Difficult Position

Because being HIV-negative does not carry the same personal identification as being HIV-positive, and given the merger of HIV and gay men's identification with the epidemic, it is essential that uninfected men are able to find a fit and a place within the gay community. This fit needs to occur without becoming infected with HIV. Being an HIV-negative gay man is a very difficult position to be in and even more difficult to describe. It does not provide the same type of container as being HIV-positive. This is partly responsible for the phenomenon of many gay men feeling it might be easier to "just become infected and get it over with."

> *Carl Locke, "Coming Out in the AIDS Era:*
> *One HIV-Negative Gay Man's Story,"*
> The HIV-Negative Gay Man:
> Developing Strategies for Survival and Emotional Well-Being,
> *ed. Steven Ball. New York: Haworth Press, 1998.*

An Ongoing Challenge

Is it, as some suggest, time to resurrect clunking-fist campaigns?

Alan Wardle, head of health promotion at the Terrence Higgins Trust, denies the suggestion that campaigns are too soft. "We try to give people the best information we can to make the best choice they can. But it is an ongoing challenge—there are only so many different ways you can say 'use a condom'. We know from the anti-smoking campaigns that fear isn't enough to stop people doing it."

He says the number of people with HIV in this country continues to grow with groups most at risk being gay men and black Africans of both sexes. But he defends the young gay generation against accusations of recklessness. "There's this notion that there's a whole host of young, gay men dispensing with condoms and thinking it's a risk worth taking but I don't think there's the evidence to back it up." Though contracting HIV is "not the death sentence it used to be", he says, "you will be putting quite toxic medicine into your body for the rest of your life and HIV is still quite highly stigmatised."

Some think that "dread ad" campaigns are self-defeating and that the issue is too complex for a sledgehammer approach.

Trevor Hoppe, an American academic specialising in sexuality and sociology and a well-known voice in health activism in the United States, believes that public health scare tactics have in some cases caused a backlash. He says: "This isn't the perspective of the majority of gay men, by far, but a minority who are very vocal and proud of their rejection of HIV prevention. I believe that is their right, and at the same time I think it is the product of abstinence-only, fear-mongering health promotion that laid the Orwellian [a totalitarian society controlling the public and private activities of its citizens, as portrayed in George Orwell's novel 1984] foundation for such a visceral and at times militant resistance."

Hoppe says that for today's young gay men "AIDS just isn't their starting point for understanding their sexualities. That doesn't mean that they are careless about HIV—on the contrary, my research with young gay men suggests that they're well aware of HIV and do what they can to avoid contracting it. This varies geographically, of course.

"I'm shocked to discover that my students—both gay and straight—at the University of Michigan often have little idea of how HIV is transmitted. The less information they have, the more scared they are about HIV. They are a product of [President George W.] Bush-era abstinence-only education, and they are totally clueless. That is a tragedy."

Some believe that another price to pay for a new HIV epidemic would be a return to the dark days of extreme prejudice.

"Gay people feel no different from straight people which is great in terms of how times have changed," says Jonathan Harvey. "But I don't think homophobia has disappeared in the same way that I don't think racism has disappeared. It's just that the gay community has become visible and strong and is answering back. But it doesn't mean that a boy comes out of a club and doesn't get beaten up."

As the older man in *Canary* says, if the young heed the safe sex warning and stay healthy then the wretched, skeletal souls we remember from the 1980s won't have died for nothing.

I *"HIV continues to be misrecognized as a disease of gay debauchery."*

The HIV Problem for Gay Men Is Distorted

Tony Valenzuela

In the following viewpoint, Tony Valenzuela asserts gay and bisexual men are unfairly portrayed as sexually promiscuous and irresponsible in discussions of HIV and AIDS. He insists that this group has similar rates of unprotected sex as heterosexuals but that several factors increase the risk for the former. He states that anal sex is more conducive to HIV transmission than vaginal intercourse. Moreover, Valenzuela claims that gay black men have the highest HIV rates because of inadequate health care and their sexual partners are usually other black men. Unprotected gay sex, he puts forth, is framed as a social and mental problem, not a practice for greater sexual pleasure and intimacy. Valenzuela writes about sex and gay issues and is the author of Unprotected.

As you read, consider the following questions:

1. What attitudes did the media have toward the New York Patient, according to the author?

Tony Valenzuela, "Killer Gay Sex!" *POZ*, May 7, 2008. Reproduced by permission.

2. As described by the author, how do sex roles account for the different rates of HIV transmission between homosexuals and heterosexuals?

3. What would reduce HIV transmissions, in Valenzuela's opinion?

In February 2005, a New York man with a multidrug-resistant strain of HIV [human immunodeficiency virus] and a crystal meth dependency became the source of the most reported AIDS [acquired immune deficiency syndrome] story of the decade, but he had never, until now [in 2008], spoken about his trying ordeal. A slew of chilling claims was made about this man—that he carried a new, more virulent strain of HIV dubbed a "supervirus" that progressed from infection to AIDS in as little as two months; that his meth-induced promiscuity would instigate a deadly epidemic potentially undoing a quarter century of progress against HIV; that he signified what many in the gay community had been dreading would occur, given that gay men—stubbornly, recklessly—refused to give up their uniquely nefarious brand of promiscuity. It is, then, no less remarkable that these allegations that gripped the world with renewed fears of gay plague proved comprehensively false, yet the cycle of alarm that equates gay men with disease—as seen once again this past January [2008] in San Francisco with a drug-resistant "gay staph" scare—continues unabated to this day. By the time the man with the "supervirus" disappeared from the headlines, those still paying attention would learn he did not have a never-before-seen strain of HIV nor did he set off a new epidemic. Instead, he carried a very rare and difficult-to-treat multidrug-resistant virus that is today fully suppressed as he adheres to a complicated regimen of antiviral medications.

In Paris, the same year the "supervirus" story broke, the late gay rights pioneer and scholar Eric Rofes declared to an audience of international activists, "The pathologizing of gay men's communities and cultures and spaces is the most powerful challenge we face to promoting gay men's health." Three years later, this man's story lays bare how far too many who work and report on gay health narrowly imagine the sex lives of gay and bisexual men inside a realm of disease and dysfunction.

"This was something that changed my life radically," the New York man told me in the thoughtful, considered tone that marked our many conversations. "I had to give up my job. I had to stay in bed. I got HIV. Sometimes I feel like I wish I had cancer so I wouldn't have to deal with the stigma that goes with this." I would speak to him only by phone at first, each of us on different coasts. He has been careful to keep his identity secret for fear, not ungrounded, that past sex partners or public health vigilantes stoked by the yellow journalism that covered his story would seek him out for retribution. In addition, he has yet to tell his family what he's been through. For these reasons, I have omitted some details of his life. Because I cannot use his real name, I will call him the New York Patient, a problematic epithet but one relevant still since he is like so many gay and bisexual men today—awash in diagnoses.

Sexually Irresponsible Gay Men?

The New York Patient was terrified and weak when the news of his virus broke on February 11, 2005. In an ominous press conference declaration, Thomas Frieden, MD, commissioner of the New York City Department of Health and Mental Hygiene, announced the discovery of a strain of HIV that was "difficult or impossible to treat" and that "potentially, no one" was immune. At 46 years old, the Cuban-born man believed that he would die and bought a cemetery property in a family plot in Florida. It was an arduous yearlong climb out of precarious health, six months before his viral load fell to undetectable levels or before he could leave a bedridden life to take short, exhausting walks in his Manhattan neighborhood. Having plummeted to a dangerously low 28, his CD4 cells [a type of white blood cells in the immune system] inched upward gradually until November 2006, when they climbed above 200 where they've remained since.

The health commissioner's press conference incited terror of the return to the AIDS-as-death-sentence days of the '80s and early '90s so that the anomalous story of one man's potent infection turned into a universalizing gay morality tale. Activist Larry Kramer called the New York Patient a "total and utter asshole" in the *New York Observer* then suggested to Gay.com that "one thing is certain: We must make all efforts to de-eroticize anal sex." Historian Charles Kaiser went further, telling the *New York Times*, "A person who is HIV positive has no more right to unprotected intercourse than he has the right to put a bullet through another person's head." And Michael Weinstein, president of the Los Angeles-based AIDS Healthcare Foundation, told the *Advocate* that the New York Patient was "indicative of a subculture of self-destruction and carelessness about our health." These are just a few examples of dozens like them where the crystal meth context of the New York Patient's infection is incidental to pointed assumptions about gay sex: self-destruction, suicide and murder have been ascribed to sex between men long before meth crowded headlines.

The moral panic that ensued over the New York Patient's personal sex life was one familiar to those of us who have observed, or participated in, these paroxysms of anger since the mid-1990s, when it became clear among researchers that gay and bisexual men would not, for reasons simple and complex, use a condom every time, even though they use them far more often than heterosexuals. The trail of high-profile, high-drama explanations that have attempted to make sense of continued HIV infections often have more in common with

The Upswing

As social scientists are aware, a person's response to surveys is linked to current cultural norms. A gay man, like other people, will tell researchers what he thinks they want to hear. In the 1980s, all gay men in the media represented themselves as having 100 percent safe sex, 100 percent of the time. Today, some gay men speak openly about unprotected butt sex and debates flare over barebacking [having sex without a condom] subcultures. This new discourse makes it safer for surveyed gay men to "'fess up" and tell researchers the truth about the sex they may be having. The "upswing" could also suggest that more gay men are aware that there are lower levels of HIV [human immunodeficiency virus] in gay communities—sometimes men choose to get f---ed without condoms in circumstances where they do the mental calculations and assess that their risk of being infected is minimal.

Eric Rofes,
"Barebacking and the New AIDS Hysteria,"
Stranger (Seattle), April 12, 1999.

folklore and tabloid journalism than with sound research. For over a decade, activists have engaged in rancorous debates over barebacking [having sex without a condom], circuit parties, "gift givers" and "bug chasers", men on the down low, resurgent syphilis and of course, crystal meth, to name a few, all highlighting the complacency at best or depravity at worst of gay men in the age of HIV—and all aired in deliciously lurid detail by a mainstream news media that survives on a steady diet of spectacle. In other words, we had been through this before, over and over again.

A Dangerous Fallacy

The representation of the sexually irresponsible gay man as the driving force behind new HIV infections has been a recurring theme in both mainstream and gay media despite evidence to the contrary. According to the Centers for Disease Control and Prevention (CDC) in 2005, the year the New York Patient learned he had AIDS, rates of HIV infections nationally among Latino men were up to three times higher than among white men. Infection rates among African American men were up to eight times higher than among white men. No other group in the U.S. is affected by the HIV/AIDS epidemic as severely as black gay men. Although African Americans represent only 13 percent of the U.S. population, they account for 49 percent of new HIV infections and 50 percent of new AIDS diagnoses. In a June 2006 literature review from the *American Journal of Public Health*, researchers tested a dozen hypotheses as to why this might be among black gay men in particular, ranging from rates of unprotected sex and drug use to awareness of HIV status. What researchers found was a powerful argument contradicting public health's idée fixe that the epidemic rests on individual bad behavior. Black gay men reported less risky sex on average than white gay men and similar rates of drug use. But black men also got tested for HIV less frequently and were more likely than white gay men to be unaware of their HIV infection. They had irregular access to good health care and higher rates of STDs [sexually transmitted diseases]—all proven risk factors for HIV transmission. Perhaps most importantly, the sexual networks of black gay men tended to be other black men, increasing their chance of HIV infection among a population already challenged by high levels of HIV.

In another notable study, this one from the September 2007 edition of the journal *Sexually Transmitted Diseases*, researchers at the University of Washington, Seattle, found through two large population-based surveys that gay men had similar rates of unprotected sex as heterosexuals but that the HIV epidemic among gay men in the U.S. remained strong because anal sex is more conducive to the transmission of HIV than vaginal sex. Heterosexuals maintained the same sexual roles (male insertive and female receptive), while gay men often switched roles, giving HIV a greater likelihood for back-and-forth routes of transmission.

What does it mean that the same levels of sexual risk in heterosexuals, in gay men in general, and in black gay men specifically, result in vastly different rates of HIV infections across these groups? Structural dynamics far outweigh individual behavior in determining the American HIV epidemic. And yet the meth "party 'n' play" guy, the circuit boy, the so-called bug chaser, is almost always nameless, faceless but presumed to be a middle-class gay white urbanite with the skills and knowledge to keep himself HIV negative. If the fear over new infections is what's ostensibly behind this rapt concern, why is this "reckless" gay man paid so much attention when, by leaps, the brunt of HIV disease, the real number of men infected is above all else determined by a lack of access to health care and by poverty in the United States? HIV continues to be misrecognized as a disease of gay debauchery, which would imply that gay men of color are many times more irresponsible than gay white men, who are many times more irresponsible than heterosexuals: That's the cloaked assumption when HIV incidences are framed around sexual irresponsibility. When writer Dan Savage proposes that the state come after those who infect others with HIV "out of malice or negligence" so that the state can recoup "drug-support payments"—thousands of dollars a year for treatment to keep them alive, comparing drug costs to child support payments—he is unwittingly suggesting another layer of penalty to populations who are disproportionally at the punitive receiving end of the criminal justice system.

Am I saying reckless gay men don't exist? Of course not, but sexual irresponsibility is not a gays-only disorder. Nonetheless the burden of scrutiny and explanation weighs most heavily on gay men of all races. Arguably most HIV infections are due to negligence, as are the myriad diseases caused by smoking and overeating. We don't base health care policy on merit. Whatever tiny minority of people exists with a malicious intent to infect others with HIV, it's a dangerous fallacy to pin the thrust of infections on a willful disregard for health. . . .

Barebacking Redux

A red screen flashes a statistic: *25 percent of men with HIV don't even know they're positive.* "Come over here. We need to talk," says a gravelly voice that you recognize immediately as the no-nonsense tone of [actress/comedienne] Whoopi Goldberg. She appears in her famous shaded spectacles and an incredulous posture. "You think barebacking is cool? Are you kidding me?" she exclaims standing in front of a red, in-studio backdrop covered with various-size words and phrases such as *healthy, honesty and self-respect.* She continues, "We can stop HIV transmission. A condom says, 'I love myself.' Talking about HIV says, 'I respect you.' Love and respect, baby. That's cool." Whoopi along with [actresses] Susan Sarandon, Rosie Pérez and Amanda Peet each deliver two different 30-second public service announcements that ran in New York City in 2006 with overlapping messages about HIV, unprotected sex, crystal meth and self-love. For example, Rosie Pérez asks us, "Condom? No Condom? Is that a question?"

In fact, it is among the most germane questions concerning gay men's health whose elusive answer has mountains of research dedicated to it even if here the question is asked glibly by a straight celebrity. On an online gay men's health discussion group to which I belong, these ads were fiercely debated. One man posted, "Well, I know a few of them in fact have barebacked and have the progeny to prove it. So it is especially irritating that there seems to be no room for gay men to make a thoughtful decision not to use condoms. . . . Whoopi has unsafe sex and she gets a baby shower. I do it and I am a psychopath." And herein lies the problem: No such words as *thoughtful* and *unprotected* dare enter the U.S. HIV prevention lexicon in the same sentence. This man's reaction illustrates the crux of the protracted debate activists have had for a decade over sex and HIV that the New York Patient brought, once again, to a boiling point.

Over the years, the dialogue around unprotected sex has evolved as researchers have made it a favorite subject of study, so that what was initially seen as fringe behavior has been largely reframed as a problem, albeit a common one, of mental health. This work has produced a constellation of psychological syndromes, afflictions, deficits or social miasma to explain sex without condoms: low self-esteem, survivor's guilt, loneliness, drugs, alcohol, lust, condom fatigue, AIDS fatigue, depression, sex addiction, poverty, slipping up, homophobia, internalized homophobia, racism, invincibility, complacency, because it feels better, childhood sexual abuse, self-destructiveness, sexual compulsiveness, denial, lack of education, resignation, love and the list goes on. Yet the primary reasons both HIV-positive and HIV-negative gay men give for having unprotected sex is to feel greater physical pleasure and to feel more emotionally connected with their partners—the same reasons straight people bareback. Far less frequently, men cite a dislike of condoms, being high on drugs or alcohol or to do something taboo. Despite the formidable challenges gay men face in their lives, more often than not we embody a tremendous range of responses, strategies and successes. At the end of the day this is our story, not the list of deficiencies that have reduced us to a pre-Stonewall [the 1969 riots that sparked the gay rights movement], pre-feminist notion of the patient under the omniscient gaze of the doctor.

I won't resolve here the different points of view over bare-backing, intentional unprotected sex, natural sex, raw sex—whatever you want to call it. I don't believe there is a resolution. It is a subject deeply entangled in the normalizing politics of gay assimilation, in personal histories of grief and fear, in individuals' boundaries of safety, in their sexual ethics and sense of morality that is formed by the minutiae of experience, politics, culture, emotion, that make us who we are.

To say the least, it is challenging to speak sensibly about gay sex, especially in the United States, when one is up against powerful institutions—health, media, politics—invested in determining all risk as pathological, gay men as damaged, disease as crisis, and HIV as it used to be—a virtual death sentence—instead of what it has become for people on antiretroviral meds: a chronic disease that must be managed with regular quality health care, individualized treatment and a broad range of physical, mental and, for some, spiritual health practices to help them live as close to a normal life span as possible.

People still die of AIDS. The treatments can and often do cause mild to moderate (and less often, severe) side effects, and scientists are now identifying long-term health consequences, such as increased risk for liver and cardiovascular disease. Some activists and public health officials are convinced gay men don't know this or have forgotten or are in denial or don't care, and the proof is their continued risk taking, in increased HIV infections, drug use, depression, loneliness, (insert here long list of deficits from above). This loop starts with sexual risk and doesn't usually but sometimes does result in new HIV infections that are used to justify the pathologizing of gay sex, the deficits approach to our health, the use of disease as terror to curb the risk taking that doesn't usually but sometimes . . . and on and on.

I suggest a way out of this all too familiar vicious circle, besides the obvious demands for universal health care and fighting poverty (two social justice issues that would do more for reducing HIV infections than all behavioral interventions combined): We must stop using HIV as the primary gauge to measure the gay well and unwell. There are other health challenges, like drug abuse, mental health, obesity and smoking, that are also harming gay men and lesbians. If HIV continues to be the barometer by which we assess the wellness of gay men—instead of one among many physical, mental and spiritual health concerns—then we are destined for generations of failed gay and bisexual men, because risk will not diminish as the consequences of it do.

> As the evidence discussed in this page makes clear, however, AIDS is acting [as] a serious barrier to Africa's development.

The Impact of HIV and AIDS on Africa

Avert

Based in the United Kingdom, Avert [www.avert.org] is an international HIV and AIDS charitable organization. In the following viewpoint, Avert upholds that two-thirds of all people with HIV in the world live in sub-Saharan Africa, resulting in 1.3 million deaths in 2009. Avert states that the epidemic has crippling impacts on households, food production, education, health care, and many African nations' economies, which are worsened by the region's poor public infrastructures and poverty. While access to treatment is growing, the organization warns that many people do not receive it and HIV interventions are still lacking.

As you read, consider the following questions:

1. How has AIDS affected health care workers in Botswana, as described by Avert?

Avert, "The Impact of HIV & AIDS on Africa," Avert.org, April 8, 2010. http://www.avert.org/aids-impact-africa.htm. Reproduced by permission.

2. According to the organization, how do African households cope with HIV and AIDS?

3. What figures does Avert cite regarding the impact of
AIDS on businesses and workers?

Two-thirds of all people infected with HIV live in sub-
Saharan Africa, although this region contains little more
than 10% of the world's population.[1] AIDS has caused immense human suffering in the continent. The most obvious
effect of this crisis has been illness and death, but the impact
of the epidemic has certainly not been confined to the health
sector; households, schools, workplaces and economies have
also been badly affected.

During 2009 alone, an estimated 1.3 million adults and
children died as a result of AIDS in sub-Saharan Africa.[2] Since
the beginning of the epidemic more than 15 million Africans
have died from AIDS.[3]

Although access to antiretroviral treatment is starting to
lessen the toll of AIDS, fewer than half of Africans who need
treatment are receiving it.[4] The impact of AIDS will remain
severe for many years to come.

The Impact on the Health Sector

In all heavily affected countries the AIDS epidemic is adding
additional pressure on the health sector. As the epidemic ma-
tures, the demand for care for those living with HIV rises, as
does the toll of AIDS on health workers.

The effect on hospitals

As the HIV prevalence of a country rises, the strain placed
on its hospitals is likely to increase. In sub-Saharan Africa,
people with HIV-related diseases occupy more than half of all
hospital beds.[5] Government-funded research in South Africa
has suggested that, on average, HIV-positive patients stay in
hospital four times longer than other patients.[6]

Hospitals are struggling to cope, especially in poorer African countries where there are often too few beds available. This shortage results in people being admitted only in the later stages of illness, reducing their chances of recovery.

Health care workers

While AIDS is causing an increased demand for health services, large numbers of healthcare professionals are being directly affected by the epidemic. Botswana for example, lost 17% of its healthcare workforce due to AIDS between 1999 and 2005. A study in one region of Zambia found that 40% of midwives were HIV-positive.[7] Healthcare workers are already scarce in most African countries. Excessive workloads, poor pay and migration to richer countries are among the factors contributing to this shortage.

Although the recent increase in the provision of antiretroviral drugs (which significantly delay the progression from HIV to AIDS) has brought hope to many in Africa, it has also put increased strain on healthcare workers. Providing antiretroviral treatment to everyone who needs it requires more time and training than is currently available in most countries.

The Impact on Households

The toll of HIV and AIDS on households can be very severe. Although no part of the population is unaffected by HIV, it is often the poorest sectors of society that are most vulnerable to the epidemic and for whom the consequences are most severe. In many cases, the presence of AIDS causes the household to dissolve, as parents die and children are sent to relatives for care and upbringing. A study in rural South Africa suggested that households in which an adult had died from AIDS were four times more likely to dissolve than those in which no deaths had occurred.[8] Much happens before this dissolution takes place: AIDS strips families of their assets and income earners, further impoverishing the poor.

Household income

In Botswana it is estimated that, on average, every income earner is likely to acquire one additional dependent over the next ten years due to the AIDS epidemic. A dramatic increase in destitute households—those with no income earners—is also expected.[9]

Other countries in the region are experiencing the same problem, as individuals who would otherwise provide a household with income are prevented from working—either because they are ill with AIDS themselves or because they are caring for another sick family member.

Such a situation is likely to have repercussions for every member of the family. Children may be forced to abandon their education and in some cases women may be forced to turn to sex work ('prostitution'). This can lead to a higher risk of HIV transmission, which further exacerbates the situation.

A study in South Africa found that poor households coping with members who are sick from HIV or AIDS were reducing spending on necessities even further. The most likely expenses to be cut were clothing (21%), electricity (16%) and other services (9%). Falling incomes forced about 6% of households to reduce the amount they spent on food and almost half of households reported having insufficient food at times.[10]

> *"She then led me to the kitchen and showed me empty buckets of food and said they had nothing to eat that day just like other days."*[11]

Food production

The AIDS epidemic adds to food insecurity in many areas, as agricultural work is neglected or abandoned due to household illness. In Malawi, where food shortages have had a devastating effect, it has been recognised that HIV and AIDS have diminished the country's agricultural output.[12] It was calculated in 2006 that by 2020, Malawi's agricultural workforce will be 14% smaller than it would have been without HIV and AIDS. In other countries, such as Mozambique, Botswana, Namibia and Zimbabwe, the reduction is likely to be over 20%.[13]

A study in Kenya demonstrated that food production in households in which the head of the family died of AIDS were affected in different ways depending on the sex of the deceased. As in other sub-Saharan African countries, it was generally found that the death of a male reduced the production of 'cash crops' (such as coffee, tea and sugar), while the death of a female reduced the production of grain and other crops necessary for household survival.[14]

Healthcare expenses and funeral costs

Taking care of a person sick with AIDS is not only an emotional strain for household members, but also a major strain on household resources. Loss of income, additional care-related expenses, the reduced ability of caregivers to work, and mounting medical fees push affected households deeper into poverty. It is estimated that, on average, HIV-related care can absorb one-third of a household's monthly income.[15]

The financial burden of death can also be considerable, with some families in South Africa easily spending seven times their total household monthly income on a funeral. Furthermore, although many South Africans contribute to some sort of funeral insurance plan, many of these are inadequately funded, and it is arguable that such financial arrangements detract from other savings plans or health insurance.[16]

Aside from the financial burden, providing home based care can impose demands on the physical, mental and general health of carers—usually family and friends of the sick person. Such risks are amplified if carers are untrained or unsupported by a home-based care organisation.

How do HIV/AIDS-affected households cope in Africa?

Three main coping strategies appear to be adopted among affected households. Savings are used up or assets sold; assistance is received from other households; and the composition of households tends to change, with fewer adults of prime working age in the households.

Almost invariably, the burden of coping rests with women. Upon a family member becoming ill, the role of women as carers, income-earners and housekeepers is stepped up. They are often forced to step into roles outside their homes as well. In parts of Zimbabwe, for example, women are moving into the traditionally male-dominated carpentry industry. This often results in women having less time to prepare food and for other tasks at home.

> *"I used to stay with the children, but now it is a problem. I have to work in the fields. Last year I had more money to hire labour so the crops got weeded more often. This year I had to do it myself."* Angelina, Zimbabwe[17]

Older people are also heavily affected by the epidemic; many have to care for their sick children and are often left to look after orphaned grandchildren. Older people left caring for the sick face the burden of providing financial, emotional and psychological support at a time when they would usually be expecting to receive more support as their energy levels drop with older age. Due to the amount of time spent caring for dependents, older people may become isolated from their peers as they no longer have the time to dedicate to their social networks that need to be fostered to prevent isolation and loneliness.

Tapping into savings if available and taking on more debt are usually the first options chosen by households struggling to pay for medical treatment or funerals. Then as debts mount, precious assets such as bicycles, livestock and even land are sold. Once households are stripped of their productive assets, the chances of them recovering and rebuilding their livelihoods become even slimmer.

The number of working adults in a family will often decrease.

"Our fields are idle because there is nobody to work them. We don't have machinery for farming, we only have manpower—if we are sick, or spend our time looking after family members who are sick, we have no time to spend working in the fields." Toby Solomon, commissioner for the Nsanje district, Malawi[18]

One of the more unfortunate responses to a death in poorer households is removing the children (especially girls) from school. Often the school uniforms and fees become unaffordable for the families and the child's labour and income-generating potential are required in the household.

"Because I'm a poor African woman, I can't raise enough money for three orphans. The one in secondary school, sometimes she misses first term because I'm looking for tuition. The others miss schools for two or three days at a time. I had a cow I used to milk, but as time went on the cow died, so I can't find any other income . . ." Barbara, Uganda[19]

The Impact on Children

It is hard to overemphasise the trauma and hardship that children affected by HIV and AIDS are forced to bear. The epidemic not only causes children to lose their parents or guardians, but sometimes their childhood as well.

As parents and family members become ill, children take on more responsibility to earn an income, produce food, and care for family members. It is harder for these children to access adequate nutrition, basic health care, housing and clothing.

Because AIDS claims the lives of people at an age when most already have young children, more children have been orphaned by AIDS in Africa than anywhere else. Many children are now raised by their extended families and some are even left on their own in child-headed households.

As projections of the number of AIDS orphans rise, some have called for an increase in institutional care for children. However this solution is not only expensive but also detrimental to the children. Institutionalisation stores up problems for society, which is ill equipped to cope with an influx of young adults who have not been socialised in the community in which they have to live. There are other alternatives available. One example is the approach developed by church groups in Zimbabwe, in which community members are recruited to visit orphans in their homes, where they live either with foster parents, grandparents or other relatives, or in child-headed households.

The way forward is prevention. Firstly, it is crucial to prevent children from becoming infected with HIV at birth as well as later in life. Secondly, if efforts are made to prevent adults becoming infected with HIV, and to care for those already infected, then fewer children will be orphaned by AIDS in the future.

To learn more, see our children HIV & AIDS page.

The Impact on the Education Sector

The relationship between AIDS and the education sector is circular—as the epidemic worsens, the education sector is damaged, which in turn is likely to increase the incidence of HIV transmission. There are numerous ways in which AIDS can affect education, but equally there are many ways in which education can help the fight against AIDS. The extent to which schools and other education institutions are able to continue functioning will influence how well societies eventually recover from the epidemic.

"Without education, AIDS will continue its rampant spread. With AIDS out of control, education will be out of reach." Peter Piol, Director of UNAIDS[20]

Fewer children receiving a basic education

A decline in school enrolment is one of the most visible effects of the epidemic. This in itself will have an effect on HIV prevention, as a good, basic education ranks among the most effective and cost-effective means of preventing HIV.[21]

There are numerous barriers to school attendance in Africa. Children may be removed from school to care for parents or family members, or they may themselves be living with HIV. Many are unable to afford school fees and other such expenses—this is particularly a problem among children who have lost their parents to AIDS, who often struggle to generate income.

Studies have suggested that young people with little or no education may be around twice as likely to contract HIV as those who have completed primary education.[22] In this context, the devastating effect that AIDS is having on school enrolment is a big concern. In Swaziland and the Central African Republic, it was reported that school enrolment fell by 25–30% due to AIDS at the beginning of the millennium.[23]

The impact on teachers

HIV and AIDS are having a devastating effect on the already inadequate supply of teachers in African countries; for example, a study in South Africa found that 21% of teachers aged 25–34 were living with HIV.[24]

Teachers who are affected by HIV and AIDS are likely to take periods of time off work. Those with sick families may also take time off to attend funerals or to care for sick or dying relatives, and further absenteeism may result from the psychological effects of the epidemic.[25]

When a teacher falls ill, the class may be taken on by another teacher, may be combined with another class, or may be left untaught. Even when there is a sufficient supply of teachers to replace losses, there can be a significant impact on the students. This is particularly concerning given the important role that teachers can play in the fight against AIDS.

The illness or death of teachers is especially devastating in rural areas where schools depend heavily on one or two teachers. Moreover, skilled teachers are not easily replaced. Tanzania has estimated that it needs around 45,000 additional teachers to make up for those who have died or left work because of

HIV and AIDS. The greatest proportion of staff that have been lost, according to the Tanzania Teacher's Union, were experienced staff between the ages of 41 and 50.[26]

The Impact on Enterprises and Workplaces

HIV and AIDS dramatically affect labour, setting back economic and social progress. The vast majority of people living with HIV in Africa are between the ages of 15 and 49—in the prime of their working lives.

AIDS damages businesses by squeezing productivity, adding costs, diverting productive resources, and depleting skills. Company costs for health-care, funeral benefits and pension fund commitments are likely to rise as the number of people taking early retirement or dying increases. Also, as the impact of the epidemic on households grows more severe, market demand for products and services can fall. The epidemic hits productivity through increased absenteeism. Comparative studies of East African businesses have shown that absenteeism can account for as much as 25–54% of company costs.[27]

A study in several Southern African countries has estimated that the combined impact of AIDS-related absenteeism, productivity declines, health-care expenditures, and recruitment and training expenses could cut profits by at least 6–8%.[28] Another study of a thousand companies in Southern Africa found that 9% had suffered a significant negative impact due to AIDS. In areas that have been hit hardest by the epidemic, it found that up to 40% of companies reported that HIV and AIDS were having a negative effect on profits.

Some companies, though, have implemented successful programmes to deal with the epidemic. An example is the gold-mining industry in South Africa. The gold mines attract thousands of workers, often from poor and remote regions. Most live in hostels, separated from their families. As a result a thriving sex industry operates around many mines and HIV is common. In recent years, mining companies have been

Not Inevitable

If, by 2025, millions of African people are still becoming infected with HIV each year, . . . it will not be because there was no choice. It will not be because there is no understanding of the consequences of the decisions and actions being taken now, in the early years of the century. It is not inevitable. . . .

It will be because the lessons of the first 20 years of the epidemic were not learned, or were not applied effectively. It will be because, collectively, there was insufficient political will to change behaviour (at all levels, from the institution, to the community, to the individual) and halt the forces driving the AIDS epidemic in Africa.

UNAIDS,
AIDS in Africa: Three Scenarios to 2025,
January 2005.

working with a number of organisations to implement prevention programmes for the miners. These have included mass distribution of condoms, medical care and treatment for sexually transmitted diseases, and awareness campaigns. Some mining companies have started to replace all-male hostels with accommodation for families, in order to reduce the transmission of HIV and other sexually transmitted diseases.[29]

In Swaziland, an employers' anti-AIDS coalition has been set up to promote voluntary counselling and testing. The coalition not only includes larger companies but also small and medium sized enterprises.[30] In Botswana, the Debswana diamond company offers all employees HIV testing, and provides antiretroviral drugs to HIV positive workers and their spouses.[31] This policy was introduced in 1999 when the company found that many of their workforce were HIV positive.

With a skilled workforce, it is financially worth their while to protect the health and therefore the productivity of their workers. Nevertheless, workplace programmes for HIV treatment and prevention remain scarce in Africa.[32]

The Impact on Life Expectancy

In many countries of sub-Saharan Africa, AIDS is erasing decades of progress in extending life expectancy. In the worst affected countries, average life expectancy has fallen by twenty years because of the epidemic.[33] Life expectancy at birth in Swaziland is just 31 years—less than half of what it would be without AIDS.[34]

The impact that AIDS has had on average life expectancy is partly attributed to child mortality, as increasing numbers of babies are born with HIV infections acquired from their mothers. The biggest increase in deaths, however, has been among adults aged between 20 and 49 years. This group now accounts for 60% of all deaths in sub-Saharan Africa, compared to 20% between 1985 and 1990, when the epidemic was in its early stages.[35] By affecting this age group so heavily, AIDS is hitting adults in their most economically productive years and removing the very people who could be responding to the crisis.

The Economic Impact

Through its impacts on the labour force, households and enterprises, AIDS has played a significant role in the reversal of human development in Africa.[36] One aspect of this development reversal has been the damage that the epidemic has done to the economy, which, in turn, has made it more difficult for countries to respond to the crisis.

One way in which AIDS affects the economy is by reducing the labour supply through increased mortality and illness. Amongst those who are able to work, productivity is likely to decline as a result of HIV-related illness. Government income also declines, as tax revenues fall and governments are pressured to increase their spending to deal with the expanding HIV epidemic.

The abilities of African countries to diversify their industrial base, expand exports and attract foreign investment are integral to economic progress in the region. By making labour more expensive and reducing profits, AIDS limits the ability of African countries to attract industries that depend on low-cost labour and makes investments in African businesses less desirable.[37]

The impact that AIDS has had on the economies of African countries is difficult to measure. The economies of the worst affected countries were already struggling with development challenges, debt and declining trade before the epidemic started to affect the continent. AIDS has combined with these factors to further aggravate the situation. It is thought that the impact of AIDS on the gross domestic product (GDP) of the worst affected countries is a loss of around 1.5% per year; this means that after 25 years the economy would be 31% smaller than it would otherwise have been.[38]

The Future Impact of HIV/AIDS

This page has outlined just some of the ways in which the AIDS epidemic has had a significant impact on countries in sub-Saharan Africa. Although both international and domestic efforts to overcome the crisis have been strengthened in recent years, the people of sub-Saharan Africa will continue to feel the effects of HIV and AIDS for many years to come. It is clear that as much as possible needs to be done to minimise this impact.

As access to treatment is slowly expanded throughout the continent, millions of lives are being extended and hope is being given to people who previously had none. Unfortunately though, the majority of people in need of treatment are still not receiving it, and campaigns to prevent new infections (which must remain the central focus of the fight against AIDS) are lacking in many areas.

The impact of AIDS in Africa is linked to many other problems, such as poverty and poor public infrastructures. Efforts to fight the epidemic must take these realities into account, and look at ways in which the general development of Africa can progress. As the evidence discussed in this page makes clear, however, AIDS is acting [as] a serious barrier to Africa's development. Much wider access to HIV prevention, treatment and care services is urgently needed.

Notes

1. UNAIDS (2010) 'UNAIDS report on the global AIDS epidemic *(http://www.unaids.org/globalreport/Global_report .htm)*'

2. UNAIDS (2010) 'UNAIDS report on the global AIDS epidemic *(http://www.unaids.org/globalreport/Global_report. htm)*'

3. UNAIDS (2008) 'Report on the global AIDS epidemic' *(http://www.unaids.org/en/KnowledgeCentre/HIVData/ GlobalReport/2008/)*

4. WHO/UNAIDS/UNICEF (2009) 'Towards universal access: Scaling up priority HIV/AIDS interventions in the health sector' *(http://www.who.int/hiv/pub/2009progressreport/en/ index.html)*

5. UNAIDS (2006) 'Report on the global AIDS epidemic *(http://www.unaids.org/en/HIV_data/2006GlobalReport/ default.asp)*', chapter 4: The impact of AIDS on people and societies

6. Inter Press Service News Agency (May 2006) 'Health South Africa: a burden that will only become heavier' *(http:// www.ipsnews.net/africa/nota.asp?idnews=33396)*

7. UNAIDS (2006) 'Report on the global AIDS epidemic *(http://www.unaids.org/en/HIV_data/2006GlobalReport/ default.asp)'*, chapter 4: The impact of AIDS on people and societies

8. Hosegood V., McGrath N et al. (2004), 'The impact of adult mortality on household dissolution and migration in rural South Africa', *(http://www.ncbi.nlm.nih.gov/pubmed/ 15238777?ordinalpos=18&itool=EntrezSystem2.PEntrez.Pub med.Pubmed_ResultsPanel.Pubmed_DefaultReportPanel.Pub med_RVDocSum)* AIDS, July 23rd, Vol. 18, issue 11

9. UNAIDS (2006) 'Report on the global AIDS epidemic' *(http://www.unaids.org/en/HIV_data/2006GlobalReport/ default.asp)*, chapter 4: The impact of AIDS on people and societies

10. The Henry J. Kaiser Family Foundation (October 2002), 'Hitting Home: How Households Cope with the Impact of the HIV/AIDS Epidemic' *(http://www.kff.org/southafrica/ 20021125a-index.cfm)*

11. The Henry J. Kaiser Family Foundation (October 2002), 'Hitting Home: How Households Cope with the Impact of the HIV/AIDS Epidemic' *(http://www.kff.org/southafrica/ 20021125a-index.cfm)*

12. bbc.co.uk (October 2005), 'Malawi issues food crisis appeal' *(http://news.bbc.co.uk/1/hi/world/africa/4345246.stm)*

13. UNAIDS (2006) 'Report on the global AIDS epidemic' *(http://www.unaids.org/en/HIV_data/2006GlobalReport/ default.asp)*, chapter 4: The impact of AIDS on people and societies

14. UNAIDS, (2006) 'Report on the global AIDS epidemic *(http://www.unaids.org/en/HIV_data/2006GlobalReport/ default.asp)'*, chapter 4: The impact of AIDS on people and societies

15. Steinberg M. et al. (October 2002), 'Hitting Home: How Households Cope with the Impact of the HIV/AIDS Epidemic' *(http://www.kff.org/southafrica/20021125a-index.cfm)*, The Henry J Kaiser Foundation

16. Collins, D.L., and Leibbrandt, M., (2007, November), 'The financial impact of HIV/AIDS on poor households in South Africa' *(http://www.ncbi.nlm.nih.gov/pubmed/18040168)*, AIDS 21: Supplement 7

17. Food and Agriculture Organization of the United Nations (2001) Rural Women Carry Family Burdens. Focus, AIDS - A Threat to Rural Africa. *(http://wwww.fao.org/FOCUS/E/aids/aids3-e.htm)*

18. Claire Nullis, Associated Press (2005), 'Malawi Village Underscores Impact of AIDS' *(http://www.usatoday.com/news/world/2005-10-18-malawivillage_x.htm)*, 18th October 2005

19. Human Rights Watch (2005), 'Letting them fail: government neglect and the right to education for children affected by AIDS' *(http://www.aidsportal.org/Article_Details.aspx?ID=879)*, Report vol. 17, No. 13 (A)

20. World Bank/UNESCO/UNAIDS Press release (2002) 'In turning the tide against HIV/AIDS, education is key', *(http://portal.unesco.org/es/ev-php-URL_ID-7195&URL_DO=DO_TOPIC&URL_SECTION=201.html)* October 18.

21. The World Bank (2002) 'Education and HIV/AIDS: A window of Hope' *(http://web.worldbank.org/WBSITE/EXTERNAL/TOPICS/EXTEDUCATION/0,,contentMDK:22032449%7EmenuPK:1342884%7EpagePK:210058%7EpiPK:210062%7EtheSitePK:282386%7EisCURL:Y,00.html)*

22. Global Campaign for Education (2004), 'Learning to Survive: How education for all would save millions of young people from HIV/AIDS' *(http://publications.oxfam.org.uk/oxfam/display.asp?K002P0142&sfl=series&stl=Joint%20Agency%20Briefing%20Papers&sort=sort_date/d&m=29&dc=37)*

23. UNAIDS (2002) 'Report on the Global AIDS epidemic' (*http:www.unaids.org/en/KnowledgeCentre/HIVData/ GlobalReport/Archive.asp*)

24. UNAIDS (2006) 'Report on the global AIDS epidemic' (*http://www.unaids.org/en/HIV_data/2006GlobalReport/ default.asp*), chapter 4: The impact of AIDS on people and societies

25. The World Bank (2002) 'Education and HIV/AIDS: A window of hope' (*http://web.worldbank.org/WBSITE/ EXTERNAL/TOPICS/EXTEDUCATION/0,,contentMDK: 22032449%7EmenuPK:1342884%7EpagePK:210058%7EpiP K:210062%7EtheSitePK:282386%7EisCURL:Y,00.html*)

26. UNAIDS (2006) 'Report on the global AIDS epidemic (*http://www.unaids.org/en/HIV_data/2006GlobalReport/ default.asp*)', chapter 4: The impact of AIDS on people and societies

27. UNAIDS (2003), 'HIV/AIDS: It's your business' (*http:// search.unaids.org/Preview.aspx?d=en&u=Publications/IRC- pub06/jc1008-business en.pdf&p=%2 fcgi-bin%2fMsmGo .exe%3fgrab_id%3d0%26page_id%3d3434%26query%3d% 2522hiv%2520aids%2520it%2520s%2520your%2520busi ness%2522%26hiword%3daids%2520business%2520hiv%25 20it%2520s%2520your%2520%26PV%3dl*)

28. UNAIDS (2003), 'HIV/AIDS: It's your business' (*http:// search.unaids.org/Preview.aspx?d=en&u=Publications/ IRC- pub06/jc1008-business_en.pdf&p=%2fcgi-bin%2fMsmGo .exe%3fgrab_id%3d0%26page_id%3d3434%26query %3d%2522hiv%2520aids%2520it%2520s%2520your%2520 business%2522%26hiword%3daids%2520business%2520hiv %2520it%2520s%2520your%2520%26PV%3dl*)

29. UNAIDS (2003), 'HIV/AIDS: 'Its your business' (*http:// search.unaids.org/Preview.aspx?d=en&u=Publications/IRC- pub06/jc1008-business_en.pdf&p=%2fcgi-bin%2fMsmGo.exe*

*%3fgrab_id%3d0%26page_id%3d3434%26query%3d%2522
hiv%2520aids%2520it%2520s%2520your%2520business%25
22%26hiword%3daids%2520business %2520hiv%2520it%
2520s%2520your%2520%26PV%3dl)*

30. IRINnews.org (April 2005), 'Business Coalition Launches HIV/AIDS Mitigation Plan' *(http://www.irinnews.org/ report.asp?ReportID-46839& SelectRegion=Southern_Africa)*

31. News From Africa (2003), 'Mining giant fights workplace HIV/AIDS' *(http://www. newsfromafrica.org/newsfrom africa/articles/art_1252.html)*

32. UNAIDS (2008) 'Report on the global AIDS epidemic' *(http://www.unaids.org/en/KnowledgeCentre/HIVData/ GlobalReport/2008/)*, Chapter 6

33. UNAIDS (2008) 'Report on the global AIDS epidemic *(http://www.unaids.org/en/KnowledgeCentre/HIVData/ GlobalReport/2008/)*', Chapter 1

34. CIA (accessed September 2009), 'The World Factbook - Swaziland *(https://www.cia.gov/library/publications/the- world-factbook/geos/wz.html)*'

35. UNAIDS (2006) 'Report on the global AIDS epidemic' *(http:www.unaids.org/en/HIV data/2006GlobalReport/ default.asp)*, chapter 4: The impact of AIDS on people and societies

36. United Nations Development Programme, Human Development Report 2005 *(http://'hdr.undp.org/en/reports/global/ hdr2005/)*, overview

37. Rosen S. et al (2004) 'The cost of HIV/AIDS to businesses in southern Africa' *(http://journals.lww.com/aidsonline/toc/ 2004/01230)*, AIDS 18:317–324.

38. Greener R. et al (November 2004), 'The Impact of HIV/ AIDS on Poverty and Inequality' in 'The Macroeconomics of AIDS *(http://www.imf.org/external/pubs/ft/AIDS/ engindex.htm)*'

> *"Newer studies commissioned by governments and relying on random, census-style sampling techniques found consistently lower infection rates in dozens of countries."*

The AIDS Epidemic in Africa Is Overestimated

Craig Timberg

Craig Timberg is a staff writer for the Washington Post. *In the following viewpoint, Timberg maintains that the United Nations (UN) overshot its estimations of the AIDS epidemic in Africa. The methodology used by UNAIDS, Timberg says, was based on infection rates among expectant mothers in prenatal care, who are more sexually active than other populations. The author claims that the revisions significantly scale back worldwide infections—with the epidemic decreasing in Africa for over a decade—which was welcomed by critics who alleged that the UN skewed the figures for more funding and political leverage.*

As you read, consider the following questions:

1. By how much did the UN overestimate the world's population infected with HIV, as reported by Timberg?

Craig Timberg, "U.N. to Cut Estimate of AIDS Epidemic," *Washington Post*, November 20, 2007. Reproduced by permission.

2. What is Helen Epstein's position on the announcement that the numbers were inflated?

3. Why are HIV infection rates lower in East and West Africa, as stated by the author?

The United Nations' top AIDS [acquired immune deficiency syndrome] scientists plan to acknowledge this week [in November 2007] that they have long overestimated both the size and the course of the epidemic, which they now believe has been slowing for nearly a decade, according to U.N. [United Nations] documents prepared for the announcement.

AIDS remains a devastating public health crisis in the most heavily affected areas of sub-Saharan Africa. But the far-reaching revisions amount to at least a partial acknowledgment of criticisms long leveled by outside researchers who disputed the U.N. portrayal of an ever-expanding global epidemic.

The latest estimates, due to be released publicly Tuesday, put the number of annual new HIV [human immunodeficiency virus] infections at 2.5 million, a cut of more than 40 percent from last year's estimate, documents show. The worldwide total of people infected with HIV—estimated a year ago at nearly 40 million and rising—now will be reported as 33 million.

Having millions fewer people with a lethal contagious disease is good news. Some researchers, however, contend that persistent overestimates in the widely quoted U.N. reports have long skewed funding decisions and obscured potential lessons about how to slow the spread of HIV. Critics have also said that U.N. officials overstated the extent of the epidemic to help gather political and financial support for combating AIDS.

"There was a tendency toward alarmism, and that fit perhaps a certain fundraising agenda," said Helen Epstein, author of *The Invisible Cure: Africa, the West, and the Fight Against*

AIDS. "I hope these new numbers will help refocus the response in a more pragmatic way."

Annemarie Hou, spokeswoman for the U.N. AIDS agency, speaking from Geneva, declined to comment on the grounds that the report had not been released publicly. In documents obtained by the *Washington Post*, U.N. officials say the revisions stemmed mainly from better measurements rather than fundamental shifts in the epidemic. They also say they are continually seeking to improve their tracking of AIDS with the latest available tools.

Among the reasons for the overestimate is methodology; U.N. officials traditionally based their national HIV estimates on infection rates among pregnant women receiving prenatal care. As a group, such women were younger, more urban, wealthier and likely to be more sexually active than populations as a whole, according to recent studies.

The United Nations' AIDS agency, known as UNAIDS [Joint United Nations Programme on HIV/AIDS] and led by Belgian scientist Peter Piot since its founding in 1995, has been a major advocate for increasing spending to combat the epidemic. Over the past decade, global spending on AIDS has grown by a factor of 30, reaching as much as $10 billion a year.

But in its role in tracking the spread of the epidemic and recommending strategies to combat it, UNAIDS has drawn criticism in recent years from Epstein and others who have accused it of being politicized and not scientifically rigorous.

Past Numbers as Well

For years, UNAIDS reports have portrayed an epidemic that threatened to burst beyond its epicenter in southern Africa to generate widespread illness and death in other countries. In China alone, one report warned, there would be 10 million infections—up from 1 million in 2002—by the end of the decade.

Piot often wrote personal prefaces to those reports warning of the dangers of inaction, saying in 2006 that "the pandemic and its toll are outstripping the worst predictions."

But by then, several years' worth of newer, more accurate studies already offered substantial evidence that the agency's tools for measuring and predicting the course of the epidemic were flawed.

Newer studies commissioned by governments and relying on random, census-style sampling techniques found consistently lower infection rates in dozens of countries. For example, the United Nations has cut its estimate of HIV cases in India by more than half because of a study completed this year. This week's report also includes major cuts to U.N. estimates for Nigeria, Mozambique and Zimbabwe.

The revisions affect not just current numbers but past ones as well. A UNAIDS report from December 2002, for example, put the total number of HIV cases at 42 million. The real number at that time was 30 million, the new report says.

The downward revisions also affect estimated numbers of orphans, AIDS deaths and patients in need of costly antiretroviral drugs—all major factors in setting funding levels for the world's response to the epidemic.

James Chin, a former World Health Organization AIDS expert who has long been critical of UNAIDS, said that even these revisions may not go far enough. He estimated the number of cases worldwide at 25 million.

"If they're coming out with 33 million, they're getting closer. It's a little high, but it's not outrageous anymore," Chin, author of *The AIDS Pandemic: The Collision of Epidemiology with Political Correctness*, said from Berkeley, Calif.

The picture of the AIDS epidemic portrayed by the newer studies, and set to be endorsed by U.N. scientists, shows a massive concentration of infections in the southern third of Africa, with nations such as Swaziland and Botswana reporting as many as one in four adults infected with HIV.

Rates are lower in East Africa and much lower in West Africa. Researchers say that the prevalence of circumcision, which slows the spread of HIV, and regional variations in sexual behavior are the biggest factors determining the severity of the AIDS epidemic in different countries and even within countries.

Beyond Africa, AIDS is more likely to be concentrated among high-risk groups, such as users of injectable drugs, sex workers and gay men. More precise measurements of infection rates should allow for better targeting of prevention measures, researchers say.

> *"The Chinese succeeded once in eradicating syphilis but that was in a very different political and social climate."*

Syphilis Is a Growing Threat

T. Hesketh, X.J. Ye, and W.X. Zhu

Earlier eradicated in China, syphilis is making a comeback claim T. Hesketh, X.J. Ye, and W.X. Zhu in the following viewpoint. According to the authors, its return poses a public health threat, because it is highly contagious and, if not treated in the long term, can lead to neurological and cardiovascular damage and even death. The authors state that rising infections are related to changing sexual behaviors, the growing sex industry, the mobility of its citizens, and the loss of universal health care. China's previous victory against syphilis demonstrates that control is possible through high involvement of the government, increased screening and treatment, and promoting awareness, they conclude. Hesketh is an academic at the Centre for International Health and Development, Institute of Child Health, University College London, England. Ye is an academic at the Institute of Social and Family Medicine, Zhejiang University, China. Zhu is an academic at the College of Law and Political Science, Zhejiang Normal University, China.

T. Hesketh, X.J. Ye, and W.X. Zhu, "Syphilis in China: The Great Comeback," *Emerging Health Threats Journal*, pp. 1–5, 2008. Reproduced by permission.

As you read, consider the following questions:

1. How did the Chinese government first eradicate syphilis, as stated by the authors?

2. What biological explanation do the authors offer for the return of the disease?

3. How has the social status of homosexuality contributed to higher rates of syphilis infections, in the authors' view?

Syphilis [a sexually transmitted disease] has been a major cause of mortality and morbidity for around 500 years. It is caused by the bacterium *Treponema pallidum*, which is transmitted sexually, from mother to foetus [fetus], and more rarely through injecting drug use. The symptoms of syphilis can be wide ranging, often being confused with other conditions, and may also be asymptomatic, making diagnosis a particular challenge. The disease classically presents in three distinct stages. The primary stage involves the formation of a genital chancre or ulcer, which is highly contagious. Around one-quarter of these cases go on to the secondary stage, which causes a range of symptoms including hair loss, fever, rashes, joint pains, and genital warts, which are also contagious. If left untreated, the condition can go on to the tertiary stage, which consists of chronic and severe neurological and cardiovascular damage leading to death. Syphilis infection during pregnancy leads to foetal loss, stillbirth, neonatal disease, and long-term deformities. The highly contagious nature of the disease makes detection and treatment crucial. Treatment is with drugs of the penicillin group, which are widely available.

There are also important interactions between syphilis and HIV [human immunodeficiency virus]. The presence of syphilis raises the viral load in HIV-infected individuals, and there is evidence that syphilis enhances the transmission of HIV.

Early detection and treatment of syphilis can, therefore, have a significant impact on the sexual transmission of HIV.

The Elimination of Syphilis

Syphilis was originally introduced to China in the 1500s by Portuguese traders. By the time figures became available in the 1940s, it is estimated that 5% of all urban dwellers and 3% of rural peasants were infected with syphilis, with over 50% of prostitutes across the country infected with the disease. Its spread was driven by a rampant commercial sex sector, and very limited available and effective treatments.

When Mao Zedong came to power in 1949, one of his top priorities was to address the massive disease burden of the impoverished population. The creation of a public health infrastructure and the provision of virtually universal access to free health care were just two of Mao's extraordinary achievements in the early years. The elimination of sexually transmitted disease (STD) was another. STDs were portrayed as a consequence of evil Western influences, fitting perfectly with the patriotic fervour of the time. By 1954, a nationwide STD control programme had been introduced. Thousands of health workers were trained to recognise the signs and symptoms of STDs, screening was introduced, and free antibiotics were made widely available. Brothels were closed and prostitutes were incarcerated for compulsory re-education programmes. All this occurred against a background of prohibition of pre- and extramarital sex, in a country that was virtually closed to the outside world. By 1964, the Chinese proclaimed that syphilis had been eradicated in mainland China. The successful campaign against STDs is one of the great public health successes in world history, showing how high-level political commitment, combined with community participation and health promotion, can eliminate a major disease.

The Return of Syphilis

China remained syphilis free for around two decades. The first cases of syphilis for over 20 years were reported in 1979 soon after Deng Xiaoping instigated his radical economic reform programme. This led the Ministry of Health to develop a surveillance system for STDs that was functioning by 1987 and continues to this day, providing valuable data on secular trends. It consists of mandatory case reporting from STD clinics and hospitals across the country. To increase the accuracy, a network of sentinel surveillance sites was also established in areas with known high rates of STDs.

This sentinel surveillance provides valuable data on trends. From 1989–1998, there was an increase in all STDs, but a massive 20-fold increase in syphilis over the time period, compared with a mere 2.6-fold increase in gonorrhoea. Incidence rose from 0.2 per 100,000 in 1989 to a peak of 6.5 per 100,000 in 1999. From 2000 to 2005, the incidence averaged 5.1–5.8 per 100,000 per year. The incidence has been consistently higher in men than in women but the gap had narrowed to around 1.3:1 in 1998 and has remained there. These figures compare with a syphilis incidence in the USA of 3 per 100,000 in 2005, up 11% from 2004, after an all-time low in 2000, with much of the increase in men who have sex with men (MSM). Other Asian nations, such as Thailand and India, are generally seeing a decline or little change in syphilis reports, although as elsewhere these almost inevitably underestimate the true incidence, because symptomatology can be non-specific, cases may be missed, and physicians (especially private practitioners) cannot be relied on to report.

Chinese sentinel surveillance also shows clear geographical differences, with higher incidences in not only the more prosperous southeastern coastal regions—Shanghai, Zhejiang, Fujian provinces—but also in poorer inland Guangxi. The mean age of people with reported syphilis was relatively old at 37 years, compared with 25–28 years in the USA. A further important finding is a very rapid rise in reports of congenital syphilis from 0.01 cases per 100,000 live births in 1991 to 19.7 in 2005. This is equivalent to 3400 cases of congenital syphilis per year. As syphilis also leads to spontaneous abortion and stillbirth, this figure certainly underestimates the total disease burden. . . .

With China's population estimated at over 1.3 billion, the burden of disease from syphilis is huge. Accurate numbers of individuals in high-risk groups are unclear, especially given that these activities are officially illegal, but estimates range from 2.8 to 4.5 million for sex workers, 1.8 to 2.9 million injecting drug users (IDUs), and 3.6 to 7.1 million high-risk MSM. There is some overlap between these groups and varying syphilis prevalence among them in different parts of the vast country. Extrapolating from estimates for 2000–2005 from [researcher CC] Lin's review, the most conservative figures would put the number of infected sex workers at 200,000, IDUs at 250,000, and MSM at 400,000.

The Reasons for the Resurgence

The underlying reason for the resurgence in syphilis in China is massive societal change. But first there is an intriguing biological explanation. This stems directly from the very success of the earlier eradication programme. It is known that syphilis infection causes an immune response, which reduces the probability of re-infection or modifies the course of the disease. A study of secular trends in syphilis incidence in the USA over a 50-year period revealed 10-year cycles of higher disease incidence, which were attributed to loss of protective immunity. It has been argued that the elimination of syphilis from mainland China for around two decades created a highly susceptible population with resulting increasing likelihood of disease transmission. The fact that gonorrhoea has not increased to the same degree lends weight to this argument, because gonorrhoea does not confer immunity in the same way. This may

Syphilis in the United States

The rate of primary and secondary (P&S) syphilis reported in the United States decreased during the 1990s and in 2000 was the lowest since reporting began in 1941. The low rate of syphilis and the concentration of the majority of syphilis cases in a small number of geographic areas led to the development of the *National Plan to Eliminate Syphilis*, which was announced by the surgeon general in 1999 and updated in 2006. The rate of P&S syphilis in the United States declined 89.7% between 1990 and 2000. However, the rate of P&S syphilis has increased each year since 2001, mostly in men, but also in women for the past four years. In 2008, 13,500 cases of P&S syphilis were reported to CDC [Centers for Disease Control and Prevention]. This is the highest number of cases since 1995 and corresponds to a rate of 4.5 cases per 100,000 population, an 18% increase from 2007. Since 2004, the rate of P&S syphilis has increased 67%. After 14 years of decline, the rate of congenital syphilis increased in 2006 and 2007. There were 431 cases of congenital syphilis reported in 2008, the same number reported in 2007.

US Department of Health and Human Services,
Sexually Transmitted Disease Surveillance 2008,
November 2009.

also explain why China has seen such a massive resurgence of syphilis when other Asian nations witnessing similar change in sexual behaviour, have not.

The social causes for the resurgence in syphilis are underpinned by the profound economic and social change in the past two decades that have resulted in a shift from a centralised, highly controlled, socialist economy to a booming, often unregulated, capitalist system. As a consequence of this, a number of changes have taken place that are now combining to drive the syphilis epidemic. These are (i) changes in sexual attitudes and behaviours, (ii) the new mobility of the population, and (iii) privatisation of the health care system with underinvestment in public health infrastructure.

Sexual attitudes and behaviours: There has been a gradual but definite shift in sexual attitudes and behaviours from the monogamous imperatives of the Mao years. The rise in syphilis itself, of course, shows that there must be increased levels of partner exchange compared with those previously observed. The fact that syphilis peaks in individuals in their late 30s also suggests that this is the result of a partner exchange after marriage (around 95% of Chinese marry in their 20s). It has been observed in China that non-monogamous sex, and, especially paid sex, is far more common as an extramarital activity than a premarital one. The growth in the sex industry over the past two decades, and especially the acceptance of sex being sold in non-traditional venues, such as barbershops and karaoke bars, has particularly contributed to the spread of syphilis. The number of sex workers is estimated to have increased 10-fold over the past two decades to the current estimate of 3–4 million. There are also concerns that the sex industry will continue to grow because of the emerging problem of excess men, which has resulted from a combination of the traditional Chinese preference for male offspring, the one-child policy, and easy access to sex-selective technology. This has led to a sex ratio of around 117 male births to 100 female births per year, with around 20 million excess men of reproductive age in the next two decades, with increased demands for commercial sex almost inevitable.

Studies of sexual behaviour among Chinese populations are still not common, partly as a hangover from the years of sexual repression, and partly because of traditional reluctance to discuss sexual issues. The few studies that address premarital and extramarital sex show that it has increased, dramatically, in some urban areas, but that traditional values persist, and China has not reached the levels of permissiveness seen in Western countries. . . .

Homosexuality, which had previously been totally unacceptable in virtually all echelons of society, is now achieving a level of acceptability in most urban areas with gay clubs and bars springing up in most cities. There is evidence too that the homosexual subculture is relatively promiscuous with 40% of the respondents in a Beijing study having more than 10 sexual partners. As homosexuality becomes more socially acceptable and less stigmatised, so syphilis may become more prevalent in this group, with obvious implications for disease control.

Population mobility: A further important driver of syphilis resurgence is the new mobility of the population with ease of movement across borders and within the country, which was almost unknown in the Mao years. This movement takes two major forms: migration on a long-term basis for work and short-term travel predominantly for business and tourism. Since the late 1980s, the Chinese government started to lift travel restrictions so that rural peasants can move to the cities to find work. The number of rural-urban migrants increased from 50 million in 1990 to 120 million in 2000, with an estimate of 160 million by 2010. It has been assumed that migrants are creating a demand for the sex industry and spreading STDs and HIV. Evidence from other countries shows that the sex industry thrives around communities of migrant workers who are predominantly men. But there is limited hard evidence that Chinese migrants are spreading STDs. . . .

Cost of health care: The third important driver of the syphilis epidemic is the collapse of universal free health care and much of the public health infrastructure, along with the introduction of economic reforms from the late 1970s. The current health system in China is largely privatised with many people, especially in rural areas, paying out-of-pocket for health care. This means that some of the most vulnerable do not seek health care, with syphilis sufferers left untreated, at risk of major health problems, and a source of its spread. For example, a study carried out in a rural area outside Beijing found that 80% of women with genitourinary symptoms did not attend for health care partly because of fear of the cost and partly because of poor understanding of the importance of the problem. In addition, privatisation has led to varying standards of health care, especially in terms of diagnostics, so that untreated infection continues to spread in the community.

Lessons to Be Learned

The Chinese succeeded once in eradicating syphilis but that was in a very different political and social climate. A return to centralised programmes that ignore the rights of individuals is not desirable or feasible in present-day China. But there are lessons to be learned from the earlier experience and a number of measures can be taken to reverse the epidemic trend.

First, there must be high-level political commitment. This was crucial to the earlier success in the 1950s. The Chinese already have demonstrated high-level commitment to improving some infectious disease control programmes, for HIV, then SARS (severe acute respiratory syndrome), and for avian influenza. Syphilis should be included in China's priorities for health.

Second, a cornerstone of the earlier success was accessible, affordable screening, and free treatment. Given the current high prevalence in certain groups, notably MSM, FSWs [female sex workers], and IDUs, screening programmes could at the very least start there. However, given the illegal and stigmatised nature of these risk behaviours, offering free screening and treatment is not straightforward, and uptake would probably be patchy. As far as population screening goes, the Chinese have just foregone a good opportunity. Until October 2003, screening for syphilis was frequently included in the then compulsory premarital examination, and treatment had to be completed before the marriage could take place. As it became voluntary, the number of couples undertaking screening has dropped dramatically. It is just starting to be recognised that the premarital examination performed a very useful public health function for screening for disease and for health promotion in young adults, and one province (Heilongjiang) has re-introduced it in its compulsory form, with other provinces also considering this course of action. Others are expected to follow. Screening of pregnant women is obviously crucial because of the devastating effects of congenital syphilis. Free screening was introduced in Shenzhen and this has proved cost-effective and sustainable, but it should be scaled up across the country.

Third, the huge resources that have been allocated to free HIV voluntary counselling and testing (VCT) programmes throughout the country should be extended to screen for syphilis. Given that the prevalence of syphilis is 10 times higher, the transmission easier, and the treatment effective, it seems extraordinary that it has been largely ignored in the huge programmes devoted to HIV. Many of these VCT centres are greatly underused at present, so to widen their remit to include syphilis could be done at low cost. This anomaly is not unique to China. It has been noted that in parts of sub-Saharan Africa individuals are treated for HIV while their syphilis is ignored.

Fourth, clearly awareness of the threat of syphilis needs to be raised. The Chinese have done an extraordinary job in this regard for HIV: Awareness of HIV is high among most population groups, especially the young. But much less is known about syphilis. Education of health providers and the general public should be the cornerstone. Promotion of condom use, especially in high-risk groups must be a key message. This is important, all the more, for FSWs who have sexual contact with large numbers of men. Condom use varies across studies and among different types of sex worker, but 'always' condom use averages at around one-third across key studies. Pilot programmes of 100% condom use in Jiangsu, Hubei, Hunan, Guangxi, and Hainan provinces have demonstrated reductions in the prevalence of syphilis in FSWs, and these programmes could be scaled up across the country. The other group that must be targeted for condom use is MSM. In the context of HIV/AIDS, considerable efforts are being made to target MSM, especially in bars and clubs, but they remain a difficult group to access, and there are no published reports about effective means of increasing condom use in MSM in China.

It has been suggested that the elimination of syphilis in the developed world is a realistic objective. With the acceleration in increase in the incidence now probably slowing in China, it is not inconceivable that with focused measures, such as those suggested, China could achieve important reductions in syphilis incidence in the near future.

Periodical and Internet Sources Bibliography

The following articles have been selected to supplement the diverse views presented in this chapter.

Jeanne Bergman	"The Cult of HIV Denialism," *Achieve*, Spring 2010.
Margena A. Christian	"Why African-American Teenage Girls Are Infected with STDs at Higher Rates," *Jet*, April 14, 2008.
Contraceptive Technology Update	"Women at Risk for HIV: What Is on the Horizon?" May 1, 2010.
Randy Dotinga	"Sex Partners Get STD Alerts by E-mail," *Washington Post*, October 21, 2008.
Michael Fitzpatrick	"AIDS Epidemic? It Was a 'Glorious Myth,'" *spiked*, August 2008.
Bernadine Healy	"Clueless on STDs, Throat Cancer, and Oral Sex," *U.S. News & World Report*, February 19, 2008.
Donald G. McNeil Jr.	"Advance on AIDS Raises Questions as Well as Joy," *New York Times*, July 26, 2010.
I-ching Ng	"Helping the Hidden Community of HIV," *Time*, August 19, 2008.
Mary Ellen Schneider	"Adolescents Face Unique Risk Factors for STDs," *Family Practice News*, May 15, 2006.
Trenton Straube	"Thou Shalt Fear AIDS," *Poz*, September 2010.
Carly Weeks	"Antibiotic Resistant Gonorrhea on the Rise," *Globe and Mail* (Canada), February 3, 2009.

OPPOSING
VIEWPOINTS®
SERIES

CHAPTER 2

How Should Students Be Educated About Sexually Transmitted Diseases?

Chapter Preface

Started by Columbia University's Health Promotion program in 1993, Go Ask Alice! is a popular question-and-
answer site frequented by students, youths, educators, and
parents alike. It is known for its candid responses to inquiries
about sexual health and sexuality that the university faculty
generates. According to the site, "team members have ad-
vanced degrees in public health, health education, medicine,
and counseling." Responses are reviewed and updated to "in-
sure high quality and accuracy."

Go Ask Alice! covers a range of concerns about sexually
transmitted diseases (STDs). To a lesbian who asked about the
risk of sex between women, it asserts that the group has "lower
risk for [STDs], including HIV, than their heterosexual and
bisexual counterparts," but "some infections are still common." A recently partnered woman wondered if it was possible to stop using condoms with her boyfriend of four weeks.
"There are many important things to consider, and ultimately
you are the only judge of what level of risk you are willing to
take," proposes Go Ask Alice!, continuing that condoms are
"very effective" in preventing STDs. A man inquired about the
dangers of protected sex with a prostitute. "Regardless of how
easy it is to catch an [STD], the risk of transmission will be
significantly lower if you follow safer sex guidelines, such as
always using condoms and dams, with all partners," it claims.
"It all comes down to activities, levels of protection, and the
level of risk a person is willing to take."

Critics, however, maintain that Go Ask Alice! is not a reliable source on sexual health. "Instead of accurate treatment of
such issues as condom effectiveness and the high health risk
of particular sexual practices, the sites are replete with exhor-
tations to adolescents to 'explore' their sexuality—ideology
rather than information," contends Chuck Donovan, senior

research fellow at the Heritage Foundation's DeVos Center for Religion and Civil Society. In the following chapter, the authors present their arguments for how STD education and prevention should be taught in the classroom.

> *"Almost 40 years of emphasis on 'safer sex' with 'values-neutral sex education,' condoms and contraception has clearly failed our young people."*

Abstinence-Only Education Is Effective

American College of Pediatricians

In the following viewpoint, the American College of Pediatricians strongly recommends abstinence-only education for youths. The college asserts that rigorous scientific studies show that abstinence education effectively reduces the rates of sexual initiation. In contrast, comprehensive sex education, the college argues, places emphasis on condom use and "safer sex" activities as failsafe strategies of protection and does not recognize the immaturity of the adolescent brain, which inhibits youths from making reasoned decisions and leaves them susceptible to the emotional tolls of sexual activity and sexually transmitted diseases (STDs). Established in 2002, the American College of Pediatricians is a national organization of physicians focusing on the health and well-being of adolescents.

American College of Pediatricians, "Abstinence Education," March 13, 2009. Reproduced by permission.

As you read, consider the following questions:

1. How does an STD emotionally burden adolescents, in the college's view?

2. According to the American College of Pediatricians, what does abstinence education state about condoms?

3. What are the consequences of "outercourse," as described by the college?

The American College of Pediatricians strongly endorses abstinence-until-marriage sex education and recommends adoption by all school systems in lieu of "comprehensive sex education." This position is based on "the public health principle of primary prevention—risk avoidance in lieu of risk reduction," upholding the "human right to the highest attainable standard of health."

By every measure, adolescent sexual activity is detrimental to the well-being of all involved, especially young women, and society at large. Children and adolescents from 10 to 19 years of age are more at risk for contracting a sexually transmitted infection (STI) than adults. This is due to the general practice of having multiple and higher risk sexual partners, and to the immaturity of the cervical tissue of girls and young women. The CDC [Centers for Disease Control and Prevention] recently stated that of the 19 million new cases of STIs annually reported in the United States, 50 percent occur in teens and young adults under 25 years of age. Twenty-five percent of newly diagnosed cases of HIV occur in those under 22 years of age. This translates into one in four sexually active female adolescents being infected with at least one STI.

Bacterial STIs may cause life-threatening cases of pelvic inflammatory disease (PID) and infertility. Viral STIs which include herpes, the human papillomavirus (HPV) and HIV [human immunodeficiency virus] are generally incurable. Herpes afflicts its victims with lifelong painful recurrences, may be passed on to sexual partners even when asymptomatic, and may be life threatening to infants if passed on at birth during vaginal delivery. HPV is found among 90 percent of sexually active young adults and teens. While often self-limited, HPV has high-risk strains that may persist for life and cause cancer of the cervix. HIV not only causes premature demise, but also significant suffering with lifelong dependence on multiple toxic and costly medications. The CDC estimates that STIs cost the U.S. health care system as much as $15.3 billion dollars annually.

Adolescent pregnancy is similarly associated with adverse socioeconomics that have an impact on the family, community, and society at large. One in thirteen high school girls becomes pregnant each year. Adolescent pregnancy results in decreased educational and vocational opportunities for the mothers, an increased likelihood of the family living in poverty, and significant risk for negative long-term outcomes for the children. For example, children of adolescent mothers are more likely to be born prematurely and at a low birth weight; suffer from poor health; perform poorly in school; run away from home; be abused or neglected; and grow up without a father.

Even if sexually active teens escape acquiring sexually transmitted infections (STIs) and becoming pregnant, few remain emotionally unscathed. Overall, one in eight teens suffers from depression, and suicide has risen to become the third leading cause of death for adolescents, paralleling the rise in STIs within this population. Infection with an STI has long been recognized as a cause for depression among teens. More recently, however, adolescent sexual activity alone has been acknowledged as an independent risk factor for developing low self-esteem, major depression, and attempting suicide. In studies that controlled for confounding factors, sexually active girls were found to be three times as likely to report being depressed and three times as likely to have attempted suicide when compared to sexually abstinent girls. Sexually active boys were more than twice as likely to suffer from depression and seven times as likely to have attempted suicide when compared to sexually abstinent boys. This is not mere coincidence. Scientists now know that sexual activity releases chemicals in the brain that create emotional bonds between partners. Breaking these bonds can cause depression and make it harder to bond with someone else in the future.

The Only 100 Percent Protection

Sexual activity is defined as genital contact. This includes mutual masturbation, as well as oral, vaginal, and anal intercourse. While only vaginal intercourse may result in pregnancy, all of these practices may spread STIs and lead to emotional trauma. Abstaining from all sexual activity is the only 100 percent safe and effective way to avoid teen pregnancies, STIs, and the emotional fallout of adolescent sexual activity. Almost 40 years of emphasis on "safer sex" with "values-neutral sex education," condoms and contraception has clearly failed our young people. Abstinence education does not occur in a vacuum, making it especially difficult to separate its influence from the opposing influence of the media and cultural milieu. Nevertheless, effectiveness of abstinence sex education in delaying the onset of sexual debut has been demonstrated in rigorous scientific studies. For example, five out of seven programs recently reviewed showed a significant reduction in sexual initiation rates (two programs showed rates decreased by half). Evaluation of community-based abstinence programs in peer-reviewed journals showed that they are effective in significantly reducing pregnancy. According to an April 2008 report by the Heritage Foundation "fifteen studies examined abstinence programs and eleven reported positive findings of delayed sexual initiation." Reviews by the Institute for Research & Evaluation state that "several well-designed evaluations of abstinence programs have found significant long-term reductions in adolescent sexual activity." These do not begin to thoroughly evaluate the hundreds of ongoing programs.

In its endorsement of abstinence-based sex education, the college calls attention to the scientific controversies surrounding alternative educational platforms. Most sex education curricula fall into two categories, *abstinence-until-marriage* or *comprehensive sex education programs* (occasionally also referred to as "abstinence plus" programs). Recently, abstinence education has been criticized for not providing critical health information about condom use. Abstinence education curricula, however, do not discourage the use of condoms; rather they note that chastity obviates the need for condoms. Abstinence education programs do not claim that condoms have no place in preventing STIs. Comprehensive programs, on the other hand, are misleading in the emphasis they place on condom use. These programs give teens the impression that condoms make sexual activity safe. In reality, there has been much conflicting medical literature on the effectiveness of condoms in preventing STIs since the 2000 NIH [National Institutes of Health] report on the subject and much of the controversy remains unresolved. Teens must be informed that condoms do not offer complete protection from either pregnancy or STIs.

The college position supporting abstinence-until-marriage education, unlike alternative education platforms, also recognizes the unique neurobiology of adolescent brains. The frontal cortex of the adolescent brain is still in development and unable to make the consistently wise executive decisions necessary to control action based on emotional input. Researcher Jay Giedd and others have found that young people do not have the physical brain capacity to make fully mature decisions until their mid-twenties.

Mixed Messages

Consequently, when it comes to sex education, adolescents need to be given clear direction repeatedly, as is done with

Adolescents and Condom Use

After 20-plus years of comprehensive sex education efforts in the U.S., adolescent rates of consistent condom use are not high enough to eliminate the STDs [sexually transmitted diseases] for which condoms *are* most preventive, such as HIV [human immunodeficiency syndrome], let alone STDs for which condoms are least preventive. Adolescents contract one-fourth of all new HIV infections. Among sexually active U.S. teens, only 47.8% of males and 27.5% of females report using condoms consistently over a one-year period. Efforts to improve those rates have not proven successful.

Institute for Research & Evaluation,
"'Abstinence' or 'Comprehensive' Sex Education?" June 8, 2007.

programs that address smoking, drugs, and alcohol use. Emphasis on contraceptive methods undermines the authority of parents and the strength of the abstinence message. This approach reinforces the ubiquitous (yet erroneous) message presented by the media that engaging in sexual activity is not only expected of teens, but also the norm. Adolescent brains are not equipped to handle these mixed messages. Parents and teachers need to "function as a surrogate set of frontal lobes, an auxiliary problem solver" for their teens, setting firm and immutable expectations. Adolescents need repetitive, clear, and consistent guidance.

As families address this issue of sex education, the American College of Pediatricians recommends that parents be fully aware of the content of the curriculum to which their children are being exposed. The national "Guidelines for Comprehensive Sex Education" that were drafted by the Sexuality Information and Education Council of the United States

(SIECUS) place strong emphasis on "values neutral" sex education beginning in *kindergarten*. According to these guidelines, children between the ages of 5 to 8 should be taught not only the anatomically correct names of all body parts, but also the definitions of sexual intercourse and masturbation.

Overall, these comprehensive programs only emphasize "safer sex." Many comprehensive programs also provide sexually erotic material to teens with explicit condom demonstrations. Other programs suggest alternative types of sexually stimulating contact (referred to as "outercourse") that would not result in pregnancy but still could result in STIs. Some of these activities, depending on the ages of those involved and the state in which they occur, could actually be illegal. These education programs can break down the natural barriers of those not yet involved in sexual activity and encourage experimentation. Additionally, many programs emphasize that teens do not need parental consent to obtain birth control and that teens therefore need not even discuss the issue with them.

Discouraging parental involvement eliminates one of the most powerful deterrents to sexual activity, namely, communication of parental expectations. Firm statements from parents that sex should be reserved for marriage have been found to be very effective in delaying sexual debut. Parental example and "religiosity" have also been found to be similarly protective. Adolescents reared by parents who live according to their professed faith and are actively involved in their worship community, are more likely to abstain from sexual activity as teens. Successful sex education programs involve parents and promote open discussion between parents and their children.

The State of Funding

The American College of Pediatricians also believes parents should be aware of the current state of funding and government involvement in sex education choices. Comprehensive programs receive seven to twelve times the funding of abstinence programs. However, according to a recent study by the Department of Health and Human Services [HHS], comprehensive programs do not give equal time to abstinence.

In 2004 Congressman Henry Waxman of California presented a report before Congress critical of the medical accuracy of abstinence education curricula. The Mathematica study was similarly critical of the medical accuracy of abstinence education programs. However, in 2007 the U.S. Department of Health and Human Services conducted an extensive review of nine comprehensive sex education curricula using the same methods employed by Congressman Waxman and the Mathematica study. These comprehensive programs were found to have no better record for medical accuracy. The HHS review also found that the comprehensive programs were hardly comprehensive. The amount of discussion dedicated to "safer sex" exceeded that spent on abstinence by a factor of up to seven. Some of the programs failed to mention abstinence altogether. None of the programs carefully distinguished between reducing and eliminating the risks of sexual activity, and nearly every program failed to mention the emotional consequences of early sexual activity. Although some of the comprehensive programs showed a small effect in reducing "unprotected" sex (seven of nine programs) and to a lesser extent in delaying sexual debut (two of eight programs), the impact did not extend beyond six months.

According to a 2004 Zogby poll, 90% of adults and teens agree with the American College of Pediatricians' position that teens should be given a strong abstinence message. Programs that teach sexual abstinence until marriage are about much more than simply delaying sexual activity. They assist adolescents in establishing positive character traits, formulating long-term goals, and developing emotionally healthy relationships. These programs increase the likelihood of strong marriages and families—the single most essential resource for the strength and survival of our nation.

> "Considerable scientific evidence shows that certain programs that include information about both abstinence and contraception help teenagers delay the onset of sexual activity, reduce their number of sexual partners and increase contraceptive use when they do become sexually active."

Abstinence-Only Education Is Ineffective

Cory Richards

Cory Richards is editor of The Guttmacher Report on Public Policy. *He also writes about sexual and reproductive health-related topics. In the following viewpoint, Richards opposes sex education programs that only teach abstinence as a way for protection from sexually transmitted diseases (STDs) and pregnancy. He believes that although abstinence is the only 100 percent guaranteed way to prevent pregnancy and STDs, it can and does fail. Contraceptives are effective and radically reduce the risk of disease and pregnancy among those who are sexually active. Ultimately, Richards contends that considerable evidence*

Cory Richards, "Q: Should Congress Be Giving More Financial Support to Abstinence-Only Sex Education? NO: Withholding Information About Contraception and Teaching Only Abstinence Puts Sexually Active Teens at Risk," *Insight on the News*, November 10, 2003. Reproduced by permission.

has shown that programs including information on contraception and abstinence reduce the number of sexual partners among teenagers and "delay the onset of sexual activity."

As you read, consider the following questions:

1. As stated in the article, how many women and men have had sexual intercourse by their eighteenth birthday?

2. According to Richards, what do the "great majority of sex-education teachers think that instruction should cover"?

3. How do abstinence-only programs "undermine students' confidence in contraception" as stated by Richards?

Helping young people to understand the benefits of delaying sexual activity and to resist peer pressure is, and clearly should be, a cornerstone of sex education in the United States. Virtually no one disputes the importance of abstinence education. But support for abstinence-only education which ignores or actually denigrates the effectiveness of contraceptives and condoms is not based on scientific evidence; rather it is driven by a subjective moral and, for many, religious agenda. The nation's leading medical, public-health and educational organizations endorse sex education that includes positive messages about the value of delaying sexual activity along with information about condoms and contraceptive use to avoid sexually transmitted diseases (STDs) and unintended pregnancy. Public-opinion polls show that this also is the position of parents, teachers and young people themselves in the United States.

What Does the Evidence Show?

- Teenagers and young adults are at risk of unintended pregnancies and STDs for almost a decade between the time they initiate sexual activity and when they get married. By their 18th birthday, six in 10 teenage women and nearly seven in 10 teenage men have had sexual intercourse.

- Teenage pregnancy happens. Nearly 900,000 American teenagers (ages 15–19) become pregnant each year, and almost four in five (78 percent) of these pregnancies are unintended.

- Other countries do better. Despite recent declines, the United States has one of the highest teenage pregnancy rates in the developed world. US teenagers are twice as likely to become pregnant as teenagers in England, Wales or Canada and nine times as likely as those in the Netherlands and Japan.

- Teenagers and young adults are at risk of STDs and HIV/AIDS. Four million teenagers acquire an STD annually. Half of the 40,000 new cases of HIV infection in the United States each year occur to individuals younger than age 25. This means that every hour of every day an average of two young people become infected with HIV.

- Contraceptives and condoms are effective. While it is true that successfully abstaining from sexual activity is the only 100 percent guaranteed way of preventing pregnancy and disease, abstinence can and does fail. Extensive research demonstrates that correct and consistent use of contraceptives, including condoms, radically reduces one's risk of pregnancy and disease among those who are sexually active.

Abstinence Education Does Not Provide Complete Information

Despite the clear need to help young people make safe decisions regarding sexual activity so that they can delay the initiation of sexual intercourse and protect themselves from unintended pregnancy and STDs when they become sexually active, US policy makers continue to promote school-based, abstinence-until-marriage education that fails to provide accurate and complete information about condoms or other contraceptives.

Overall, federal and matching funding from states for abstinence education that excludes information about contraception has totaled more than $700 million since 1996. There is, on the other hand, no federal program dedicated to supporting comprehensive sex education. Federal law contains an extremely narrow eight-point definition of abstinence-only education that sets forth specific messages to be taught, including that sex outside of marriage for people of any age is likely to have harmful physical and psychological effects. Because funded programs must promote abstinence exclusively, they are prohibited from advocating contraceptive use. They thus have a choice: They either must refrain from discussing contraceptive methods altogether or limit their discussion to contraceptive failure rates. Further, in many cases federal law prevents these programs from using their private funds to provide young people with information about contraception or safer-sex practices. Yet even today, many policy makers remain unfamiliar with this extremely restrictive brand of abstinence-only education required by federal law.

Considerable scientific evidence shows that certain programs that include information about both abstinence and contraception help teenagers delay the onset of sexual activity, reduce their number of sexual partners and increase contraceptive use when they do become sexually active. Indeed, leading medical, public-health and educational organizations, including the American Medical Association, the American Academy of Pediatrics, the American College of Obstetricians and Gynecologists and the National Institutes of Health, support sex-education programs that both stress abstinence and teach young people about the importance of protecting themselves against unintended pregnancy and disease when they become sexually active.

In contrast, there have been few rigorous evaluations of programs focusing exclusively on abstinence. None of these has found evidence that these programs either delay sexual activity or reduce teen pregnancy. Finally, research on virginity-pledge programs and HIV-prevention efforts suggests that education and strategies that promote abstinence but withhold information about contraceptives (and condoms, in particular) may have harmful health consequences by deterring the use of contraceptives when teens become sexually active.

Despite similar levels of sexual activity among American teenagers and their counterparts in other developed countries, teenagers in this country fare worse in terms of pregnancy and STDs. US teenagers are less likely to use contraceptives, particularly the pill or other highly effective hormonal methods. US teenagers also have shorter relationships and thus more sexual partners over time, increasing their risk for STDs. Evidence from other developed countries, moreover, suggests that when teenagers are provided with comprehensive education about pregnancy and STD prevention in schools and community settings, levels of teenage pregnancy, childbearing and STDs are low. Adults in these other countries give clear and unambiguous messages that sex should occur within committed relationships and that sexually active teenagers are expected to take steps to protect themselves and their partners from pregnancy and STDs.

Sex Education Classes

On certain topics, there is a large gap between what sex-education teachers believe they should cover and what they actually are teaching. The great majority of sex-education teachers think that instruction should cover factual informa-

A Nationwide Trend

Twenty-three states and the District of Columbia are no longer accepting funds under the Title V abstinence-only education program.

■DC

■ Not accepting funds

TAKEN FROM: Sexuality Information and Education Council of the United States, 2009.

tion about birth control and abortion, the correct way to use a condom and sexual orientation. However, far fewer actually teach these topics, either because they are prohibited from doing so or because they fear such teaching would create controversy. As a result, a startling one in four teachers believes they are not meeting their students' needs for information.

The gap between what sex-education teachers think should be covered and what they actually teach particularly is acute when it comes to contraception. Sex-education teachers almost universally believe that students should be provided with basic factual information about birth control, but one in four teachers are prohibited by school policies from doing so. Overall, four in 10 teachers either do not teach about contraceptive methods (including condoms) or teach that they are ineffective in preventing pregnancy and STDs.

What many students are being taught in sex-education classes does not reflect public opinion about what they should be learning. Americans overwhelmingly support sex education that includes information about both abstinence and contraception. Moreover, public-opinion polls consistently show that parents of middle school and high school students support this kind of sex education over classes that teach only abstinence.

Parents also want sex-education classes to cover topics that are perceived as controversial by many school administrators and teachers. At least three-quarters of parents say that sex-education classes should cover how to use condoms and other forms of birth control, as well as provide information on abortion and sexual orientation. Yet these topics are the very ones that teachers often do not cover. Finally, two out of three parents say that significantly more classroom time should be devoted to sex education.

Similarly, students report that they want more information about sexual- and reproductive-health issues than they are receiving in school. Nearly one-half of junior high and high school students report wanting more factual information about birth control and HIV/AIDS and other STDs, as well as what to do in the event of rape or sexual assault, how to talk with a partner about birth control and how to handle pressure to have sex. Young people also need to receive information sooner: More than one-quarter of students become sexually active before they receive even a rudimentary level of sex education such as "how to say no to sex."

Undermining Confidence

Abstinence-only programs also can undermine students' confidence in contraception by providing unbalanced evidence of its ineffectiveness. These programs miss the opportunity to provide students with the skills they need to use contraceptives more, and more effectively. Instead students may leave the program thinking that pregnancy and STDs are inevitable once they begin having sex.

To be sure, promoting abstinence to young, unmarried people as a valid and realistic lifestyle choice should remain a key component of sex education. But those who argue that this is the only message that should be provided to young people are misguided. The evidence strongly suggests that sex in the teenage years and certainly prior to marriage, which now typically occurs in the mid-20s is and will continue to be common, both in this country and around the world. Undermining people's confidence in the effectiveness of condoms and other contraceptive methods as a means of scaring them out of having sex is just plain wrong. Protecting our young people requires a balanced approach that emphasizes all the key means of prevention including effective contraceptive and condom use, as well as delaying sex. Ultimately, only such a comprehensive approach will provide young people with the tools they need to protect themselves and to become sexually healthy adults.

> "*Comprehensive sexuality education* emphasizes *abstinence as the best option for adolescents, but also provides age-appropriate, medically accurate discussion and information for the prevention of sexually transmitted infections and unintended pregnancies.*"

Comprehensive Sex Education Is Effective

Margaret J. Blythe

Margaret J. Blythe is a professor of pediatrics at Indiana University School of Medicine and chair for the Committee on Adolescence, American Academy of Pediatrics. In the following viewpoint, Blythe advocates comprehensive sex education for adolescents, asserting that it emphasizes abstinence while offering age-appropriate instruction to prevent sexually transmitted diseases (STDs) and unwanted pregnancies for youths who have sex. In addition, she insists that such programs are proven to delay sexual intercourse and that withholding information about condoms and safer sex leaves young people less prepared to protect themselves. Contrary to abstinence-only proponents,

Margaret J. Blythe, "Testimony of Margaret J. Blythe, MD, FAAP, FSAM, on Behalf of the American Academy of Pediatrics," Before the Committee on Oversight and Government Reform, United States House of Representatives, April 23, 2008. Reproduced by permission.

Blythe maintains that comprehensive sex education does not encourage sexual activity or promiscuity.

As you read, consider the following questions:

1. What is the author's position on abstinence-only programs?

2. How have abstinence-only policies shaped sex education, in Blythe's opinion?

3. According to the Society of Adolescent Medicine, how does abstinence fail to protect against disease and unwanted pregnancy?

My name is Dr. Margaret Blythe. I am a pediatrician and professor of pediatrics at Indiana University School of Medicine and a subspecialist in adolescent medicine. As the current chair for the Committee on Adolescence, I have been asked to give testimony regarding the position of the American Academy of Pediatrics [AAP] on abstinence education and on age-appropriate comprehensive sexuality education and evidence supporting this position. My testimony is also endorsed by the Society for Adolescent Medicine of which I am also a member.

The American Academy of Pediatrics supports age-appropriate comprehensive sexuality and reproductive health education and wants to ensure that our nation's resources are being allocated toward educational approaches that are science-based. Comprehensive sexuality education *emphasizes* abstinence as the best option for adolescents, but also provides age-appropriate, medically accurate discussion and information for the prevention of sexually transmitted infections and unintended pregnancies.

Abstinence-only programs have not been shown to change adolescent sexual behaviors according to five systematic reviews including a federally funded evaluation of Title V programs conducted by an independent research organization. In fact, abstinence-only programs are not only *ineffective* but may cause *harm* by providing inadequate and inaccurate information and resulting in participants' failure to use safer sex practices once intercourse is initiated. Specifically, one systematic review reports that using both self-reported biological and behavioral health outcomes, the abstinence-only programs did not affect incidence of unprotected vaginal sex, frequency of vaginal sex, numbers of partners, age of sexual initiation or condom use.

Two new sets of data recently released by the Centers for Disease Control and Prevention (CDC) bring additional concerns about abstinence-only education programs and really demand a change in policy for funding sexual health education for adolescents. The most recent data indicate that births to teen girls aged 15–19 years increased by 3%; this is the first increase noted in the previous 14 years of decline. As well in this past month, CDC released new data about the prevalence of sexually transmitted infections (STIs) among adolescents, especially adolescent girls. CDC estimates that one in four girls aged 14–19 has at least one STI. This means as many as 3.2 million adolescent girls are infected with human papillomavirus (HPV), chlamydia, herpes simplex type 2, or trichomoniasis. These numbers are likely to be understated because syphilis, gonorrhea and the human immunodeficiency virus [HIV] were not included in the data CDC analyzed for the estimate.

The Only Strategy?

Children and adolescents need accurate and comprehensive education about sexuality not only to practice healthy sexual behaviors as adults, but also to avoid early, exploitative or risky sexual activity that may lead to health and social problems, such as unintended pregnancy and STIs, including HIV infection and AIDS [acquired immune deficiency syndrome].

Medical Accuracy

A number of reports have examined the medical accuracy of federally funded abstinence-only programs. According to a 2004 congressional review conducted by the minority staff of the House Committee on [Oversight and] Government Reform, 11 of the 13 most popular abstinence-only curricula were rife with medical and scientific inaccuracies. For example, many grossly underestimated the effectiveness of condoms, made false claims about the risks of abortion or offered misinformation on the incidence and transmission of STIs [sexually transmitted infections]. Two more recent reviews by the Government Accountability Office found similar problems, faulting the government for not keeping closer tabs on the medical accuracy of grantees' educational materials.

Heather D. Boonstra,
"Advocates Call for a New Approach After
the Era of 'Abstinence-Only' Sex Education,"
Guttmacher Policy Review, *Winter 2009.*

This is especially true among gay, lesbian and bisexual youth who are more likely to have had sexual intercourse, to have had more partners, and to have experienced sexual intercourse against their will, putting them at increased risk of STIs including HIV infection. The data is clear that abstinence is the most effective means of birth control and prevention of STIs and needs to be included as part of an individual's strategy to reduce unintended pregnancy and STI rates. But abstinence should not be taught as the *only strategy.* To date, the evidence regarding the efficacy of abstinence-only in the reduction of risky sexual behaviors, including risk for STIs, has not been proven. For some adolescents, abstinence may be a difficult choice. And in practice, many adolescents who intend to be abstinent often fail and have sex. A longitudinal analysis of teens and virginity pledges compared "pledgers" to "non-pledgers" and found at a six-year follow-up that 88% of pledgers reported experiencing premarital sex and had STI rates that, statistically, were no different from those of non-pledgers.

Evidence suggests that abstinence-only policies of the federal government changed the nature of sexuality education in the United States with many schools adopting abstinence-dominant or abstinence-only education programs for school sexuality curricula. Data comparing 1995 to 2002 showed a decline in young women reporting education about contraception (87% to 70%) and an increase in abstinence-only education (8% to 21%) with a decrease in those receiving both (84% to 65%). Citing the ineffectiveness of abstinence-only programs, already 17 states have opted out of Title V funding. Estimates suggest over 40% of youth in the United States between the ages of 12 to 18 years live in these states. The most recent review of abstinence-only programs in 2007 by the National Campaign to Prevent Teen and Unplanned Pregnancy continue to support that such programs are ineffective at reducing risky sexual behaviors. Specifically, these programs "did not delay the initiation of sex, did not increase the return to abstinence, or decrease the number of sexual partners."

Several published studies and evaluations have suggested that *comprehensive sexuality education* is an effective strategy for helping young people delay initiation of sexual intercourse. Comprehensive programs encourage abstinence as the best option but offer discussion and education for those adolescents who are sexually active about protecting against sexually transmitted infections and contraception. Research has shown that these programs do not hasten the onset or frequency of sexual intercourse and do not increase the number of partners that sexually active teens have.

Comprehensive Education and Sexual Activity

A national study compared sexual health risks of adolescents who received abstinence-only education and those who received comprehensive sex education to those who received none. Adolescents who reported having received comprehensive sex education before initiating sexual intercourse were significantly less likely to report a teen pregnancy compared to those receiving no sexual education while there was no effect of abstinence-only education. Sexuality education and interventions with some abstinence-base or "abstinence-plus" curriculum components are most effective when targeted at younger adolescents before they become sexually active.

Providing information to adolescents about contraception does not result in increased rates of sexual activity, earlier age of first intercourse, or a greater number of partners. In fact, if adolescents perceive obstacles to obtaining contraception and condoms, they are more likely to experience negative outcomes related to sexual activity.

Adolescents who choose to abstain from sexual intercourse should be encouraged and supported by their parents, peers, pediatricians and society, including the media. Adolescents need to know about other contraceptive options before (or if) they decide to have intercourse. Based on the evidence, AAP supports a comprehensive approach to sexuality education for adolescents. Abstinence should play a part in any comprehensive discussion of sexuality, with support and resources available for adolescents who feel pressured, but prefer not, to engage in sexual activity.

From a public health perspective, primary prevention of unintended pregnancy and STIs in adolescents involves a delay in the initiation of sexual activity until psychosocial maturity or marriage, depending on the religious or cultural perspective. Secondary prevention in adolescents involves the use of safer sex practices by those who are sexually active and who do not plan on abstaining from sexual activity. Adolescence is a time of growth and change—physically, psychosocially and emotionally. Developing a healthy sexuality is a key developmental task for adolescents. With these changes and goals come a desire and a need to assert independence and take responsibility for decisions and behaviors that impact health. Evidenced-based approaches that support healthy decisions and further these goals benefit not only the adolescent as an individual but the health of our society and nation as a whole.

The Society for Adolescent Medicine summarized its expert review of sexuality education with the following:

> Abstinence from sexual intercourse represents a healthy choice for teenagers, as teenagers face considerable risk to their reproductive health from unintended pregnancies and STIs including infection with HIV. Remaining abstinent, at least through high school, is strongly supported by parents and even by adolescents themselves. However, few Americans remain abstinent until marriage, many do not or cannot marry, and most initiate sexual intercourse and other sexual behaviors as adolescents. Abstinence as a behavioral goal is not the same as abstinence-only education programs. Abstinence from sexual intercourse, while theoretically fully protective, often fails to protect against pregnancy and disease in actual practice because abstinence is not maintained.

> "Parents, if you believe that the goals of sexuality education are to prevent pregnancy and disease, you are being hoodwinked."

Comprehensive Sex Education Is Harmful

Miriam Grossman

Miriam Grossman is a physician and author of You're Teaching My Child What? A Physician Exposes the Lies of Sex Education and How They Harm Your Child. *In the following viewpoint excerpted from her book, Grossman argues that comprehensive sex education teaches sexual freedom, not sexual health. These programs instruct children—as early as preschool—about sexual expression, alternative lifestyles, masturbation, prostitution, and abnormal sexual practices, she maintains. Furthermore, Grossman contends, they gloss over the weaknesses of condoms and girls' increased vulnerability to sexually transmitted diseases (STDs). The so-called "experts" of comprehensive sex education are wrong and dismiss the findings of child development, neurobiology, and disease, Grossman concludes.*

Miriam Grossman, "Introduction: Shocked," *You're Teaching My Child What? A Physician Exposes the Lies of Sex Education and How They Harm Your Child*. Washington, DC: Regnery Publications, 2009, pp. 6–12. Reproduced by permission.

As you read, consider the following questions:

1. In Grossman's view, why are adolescents incapable of using condoms and birth control responsibly?

2. What can youths find out about on the Go Ask Alice! website, as stated by the author?

3. What messages do comprehensive programs send to students, as described by Grossman?

Objections to today's sex education are hardly new. Some parents have been active in their opposition, taking legal action, even going to jail. But organizations such as SIECUS [Sexuality Information and Education Council of the United States] and Planned Parenthood [Federation of America] claim neutrality and successfully portray the conflict as religious right versus medical facts, hicks versus Harvard.

Those hicks must be on to something, because recent discoveries in neurobiology, endocrinology, and histology indicate science is in *their* corner. I contend that it's "comprehensive sexuality education" that's animated by pseudoscience and crackpot ideology. Sexuality educators charge their opposition with censoring medically accurate, up-to-date science, and argue that kids need more than a "plumbing lesson." Yet the sex ed [education] industry is no less guilty of using science selectively and omitting facts that contradict their agendas. It's time to call foul.

SIECUS and Planned Parenthood have yet to recognize some of the most compelling research of recent years. These organizations are still animated by the philosophies of the infamous sexologist Alfred Kinsey—whose work has been debunked—the birth control and eugenics advocate Margaret Sanger, the feminist Gloria Steinem, and *Playboy* founder Hugh Hefner. These twentieth-century crusaders were passionate about social change, not health. Their goal was a cultural revolution, not the eradication of disease. And the same is true for the sex ed industry. That's why their premises haven't changed in fifty years, even as journals like ... the *New England Journal of Medicine* have [been] filled with research contradicting them.

Bizarro World

While SIECUS informs kids that culture teaches what it means to be a man or a woman, neuroscientists identify distinct "male brains" or "female brains" while a child is still in the womb. According to the "experts," a girl is a "young woman," ready for "sex play," but gynecologists know the question is not *whether* a sexually active "young woman" will get herpes, HPV [human papillomavirus], or chlamydia, it's *which one.* "Respect your teens' decisions," parents are advised; "step aside, and don't judge." But studies show kids do best when parents convey their expectations and stand firm. Give adolescents information, they promise, provide them with condoms and pills, and they'll make smart decisions. But MRIs show that during highly charged moments, teen brains rely on gut feelings, not reason. In other words, it's not ignorance causing all those pregnancies and infections; it's the unfinished wiring between brain cells.

These findings, and more, are excluded from modern sex education. Why? Because they contradict Kinsey, Hefner, and Steinem. They testify against the anything goes, women-are-just-like-men ideology. They announce to the world: Hicks–1, Harvard–0.

What Sex Ed Is Really All About

Parents, if you believe that the goals of sexuality education are to prevent pregnancy and disease, you are being hoodwinked. You must understand that these curricula are rooted in an ideology that you probably don't share. This ideology values, above all—health, science, or parental authority—sexual freedom.

According to this philosophy, a successful curriculum encourages students to develop their own values, not blindly accept those of their community. It emphasizes the wisdom they'll gain through open-mindedness and tolerance. "Students . . . become more 'wide awake' and open to multiple perspectives that make the familiar strange and the strange familiar," according to one sex education manual.

If the subject is marine biology or entomology, you might not mind if the "strange" becomes the "familiar" to your child. But when it comes to issues of sexuality, it might be another matter entirely. Do you want instructors, whose personal values might be at odds with yours, to encourage your kids to question what they've been taught at home and at church, and to come up with their own worldview based on taking sexual risks that endanger their health and well-being? It seems reasonable to question the ethics of this practice.

What these "experts" are hiding is their goal of bringing about radical social change, one child at a time. Their mission is to mold each student into what is considered "a sexually healthy" adult—as if there was universal agreement on what that is. From a review of many of today's sex ed curricula and websites, it would appear that a "sexually healthy" individual is one who has been "desensitized," who is without any sense of embarrassment or shame (what some might consider "modesty"), whose sexuality is always "positive" and "open," who respects and accepts "diverse" lifestyles, and who practices "safer sex" with every "partner."

This is not about health, folks. This is about indoctrination.

The Madness of "Comprehensive Sex Ed"

Don't wait until children ask questions, parents are told by sex education "experts"; to ensure their healthy future, they need information early. Teach preschoolers that each of us is sexual,

from cradle to grave, and that "sexual expression" is one of our basic human needs, like food, water, and shelter. Encourage their "positive body concept," by expanding games such as "Simon Says" to include private parts (*Simon says point to your ear, ankle, penis*). Explain intercourse to preschoolers; tell them they have "body parts that feel good when touched." Inform five-year-olds that "everyone has sexual thoughts and fantasies" and that "people experience sexual pleasure in a number of different ways." Teach kids about HIV [human immunodeficiency virus] before they know their ABCs.

The potential for harm is even greater a few years later when our kids must learn more, we're told, for their own good. Planned Parenthood says 3rd grade is the time to find out about wet dreams, masturbation, rape, and "sex work." Nine- to twelve-year-olds should understand that male and female are not defined solely by chromosomes or genitalia; everyone has an "internal sense" of his or her identity, and that "sense" might not jibe with what they see in the mirror.

As you can imagine, sex educators believe that the "information" teens "need" to know is more explicit and disturbing. But by then, of course, if not earlier, they can go online themselves and check out the sites sexuality educators recommend, like Columbia University's "Go Ask Alice!" I urge every adult whose life includes a young person to check out this award-winning site, one that gets over two thousand questions a week, and many more hits. On "Alice," teens find excellent information about drugs, alcohol, diet, depression, and other health issues. But they also learn how to purchase "adult products" by phone, arrange a threesome, and stay "safe" during sadomasochistic "sex play."

Yes, madness—that's the right word.

With messages like this coming from websites recommended to our kids, it should come as no surprise that 34 percent of girls are sexually active by age fifteen. The figure goes up to nearly 80 percent four years later, with more than one-fifth of all fifteen- to nineteen-year-olds reporting two or more partners *in the past year*. Hey, they are exploring their sexuality; it's only "natural."

But in these times, anyone "exploring" sexuality is at risk for some two dozen different bacteria, viruses, parasites, and fungi: and infection is likely to happen soon after sexual debut. Who suffers the most? Girls. One of the many facts withheld by "sex educators" is that teen girls are anatomically more vulnerable to sexually transmitted diseases [STDs] than boys. They also gloss over the fact that decades of sex education have taken our society from having essentially two sexually transmitted diseases to worry about (syphilis and gonorrhea) to having more than two dozen, including some incurable viruses, and one that's often fatal: HIV. They deem it vital for kids to know there are not one, but *three* types of intercourse; apparently they don't need to know that one of these is so dangerous that a surgeon general warned against it, even *with a* condom.

And this question is never, ever raised: What new bug is out there, spreading undetected, an epidemic in the making?

There are some things you need to know about condoms—what sex educators call "protection." Most teens do not use them correctly and consistently. Even with proper use, both pregnancy and infection can occur. That's why so many health providers have given unwelcome news to young patients who insist, *"But we used a condom, every time!"*

These young victims are angry, because even after following the rules, after being responsible, they're in trouble: Using a condom gave them a false sense of security. And need I mention that latex provides no protection against the emotional distress that often follows teen sexual behavior? As many have observed, condoms do not protect the heart, in particular the female heart. That's another thing SIECUS, Planned Parenthood, and Columbia's "Alice" never tell your daughter.

Again, the priority of our nation's sex educators is to promote sexual freedom, not prevent infections and emotional distress. In fact, as the numbers of infections reach ever more mind-numbing levels, these educators argue for more of last century's methods. The solution to the epidemic is to teach *more* kids they are "sexual from womb to tomb," encourage *more* teens to question their families' values, and to send trucks with even *larger* loads of contraceptives to middle schools—to be distributed without parental knowledge. Have they lost their minds?

Wake Up, America!

You might think I'm bashing sex ed because I'm on the other side of the battle. Not exactly. Abstinence education tells kids to wait for marriage, and for many that message rests on moral foundations. As an Orthodox Jew, I share those values—but you won't find me quoting Leviticus in these pages.

I'll leave that to parents and pastors. I write as a physician, and my approach is anchored in hard science.

I wrote this book [*You're Teaching My Child What? A Physician Exposes the Lies of Sex Education and How They Harm Your Child*] to tell parents they're being conned by the sex education industry. These powerful organizations present themselves as guardians of our children's health and well-being; they claim to provide kids with all the information and skills they need to make healthy choices. They assert they give your child the same message she hears at home: *you're too young—wait until you're older*. They claim their curricula are "science-based," age-appropriate, nonjudgmental, up-to-date, and medically accurate. And they believe they know better than you do what's best for your kids, so you should trust them, the "experts," and ignore your gut feelings.

Wake up, America: This is one giant hoax. I know these groups, their values, and curricula. They are *steeped* in ideology, *permeated* with extremism. Nonjudgmental? Sure, until they're challenged with scientific facts. Point to the science that discredits their beliefs, and, well, you know the names you'll be called.

They do *not* give young people the same message as parents. Children are inundated from a tender age with a "sex-positive" message; they're taught that sexuality is a lifelong adventure, "who they are" from cradle to grave, and that the freedom to explore and express their sexuality is a sacred "right." While teens are told that delaying sexual behavior is an option—and sure, it's the only 100 percent certain way to avoid infections and pregnancy—it is not presented as the healthiest choice, the one recommended by experts. Consider the views of Debra Haffner, a recent SIECUS president who is now a minister. Premarital sex is so essential, the Reverend Haffner appears to believe, that she'd "refuse to marry a couple who told me that they had shared no sexual behaviors at all."

The experts do *not* provide teens with all they need to know to make informed decisions, nor is their information medically accurate. They dismiss fundamentals of child development and omit critical findings of neurobiology, gynecology, and infectious disease. HIV information is distorted. The psychological distress associated with teen sex, especially when followed by a genital infection, is whitewashed.

The "experts" are wrong, and parents are right. Boys and girls have vast differences, sexual behavior is profound and consequential, and we reap immense benefits from self-restraint. Mom and Dad should trust their common sense, gut feelings, and traditional values. Children raised by parents who are moderately strict and voice clear expectations about delaying sexual activity are the kids least likely to engage in harmful behaviors. Yes, that throwback excuse works: *"I can't—my parents would kill me!"*

> "It's about teaching comfort with one's body, a lack of shame over desires, and that there is more to sex for all people than sticking penises inside of vaginas."

Many Sex Education Programs Are Sexist

Cara Kulwicki

In the following viewpoint, Cara Kulwicki writes that most sex education programs fail to teach that sex is pleasurable, varied, and normal and is oftentimes biased against women. Most discussions of pregnancy and sexually transmitted diseases (STDs) take place solely in the context of vaginal intercourse, she says, ignoring female anatomy and orgasm as well as other sexual acts and orientations. Kulwicki argues that this is sexist because women are not taught other ways to gratify themselves, which can help prevent pregnancy and STDs as well as help them recognize rape, coercion, and abuse. The author is the founder and executive of The Curvature, *a feminist blog, and she is a contributor to* Yes Means Yes! Visions of Female Sexual Power and a World Without Rape.

Cara Kulwicki, "The Importance of Real Sex Education," The Curvature (blog), May 26, 2008. Reproduced by permission.

As you read, consider the following questions:

1. How does the author define "real" sex education?

2. Why do discussions of sexual intercourse center around men, in the author's opinion?

3. How is teaching about pleasure in sex education different from teaching technique, in Kulwicki's view?

Those who oppose abstinence-only sex education generally promote an alternative with medically-accurate information on condoms, pregnancy, birth control and STD prevention. They may also want to include lessons acknowledging that oral and anal sex exist, that not all sex is heterosexual, and that rape is wrong.

For me, real sex education is something more. I believe that it requires actually teaching about sex. Real sex education (a phrase I will use in this way from here on) requires, in addition to teaching about protection, teaching sex as a normal and healthy part of life that is varied in terms of both preferred partners and preferred acts. Real sex education teaches that sex is more than heterosexual intercourse and should be consensual and pleasurable for all participants.

These types of suggestions are often met with resistance. We're having enough trouble fighting abstinence-only education; is now really the time to demand discussions on topics like masturbation? Even those who support medically-accurate sex education often ask the question: isn't the job of sex education to keep teenagers safe? Do we really need to teach how to give and receive pleasure? Is that even appropriate?

I absolutely understand the benefits of a gradual approach. I would much rather see teenagers learn about condoms, STDs and pregnancy prevention without learning about sexual pleasure than see them not learn about basic precautions at all. I also absolutely agree that sex education should be about keeping children, teenagers and adults sexually safe as they move through life.

But I believe that only real sex education provides all the tools needed to effectively encourage safety. And there are four basic reasons why.

Not Teaching Real Sex Education Is Discriminatory

Sex education that does not involve discussions of pleasure is innately sexist. Why? Because one can discuss pregnancy, STDs and prevention in relation to heterosexual sex without a single mention of the clitoris. Educators definitely should not do this, but the fact is that it's entirely possible to give a scientifically accurate and even practical description of birth control, condom use, vaginal intercourse, and other sex education staples without ever acknowledging its existence. And the same holds true for female orgasm.

With men, it's very different. First of all, no one ever tries to hide a man's penis from him. Secondly, in discussing intercourse and pregnancy, you can't escape the male orgasm. It has to exist for pregnancy to happen. Furthermore, in these lessons, men get a description of what is generally perceived to be the most common and/or enjoyable way to orgasm during partnered heterosexual sex. And this description—like descriptions of the most common methods of orgasming for women would—gives them a road map, if needed, to the most common masturbation techniques. When only coitus is discussed through education about pregnancy and STD prevention, women are left yet again with the impression that they are supposed to primarily derive pleasure from penetration. Of course, untold numbers of straight, lesbian and bi women love penetrative sex, and many can indeed achieve orgasm through this method. But still the fact remains that most cannot.

With this being the case, failing to teach real sex education is unacceptable. Though it's increasingly less common these days, it's entirely possible and disturbingly frequent for women to enter adulthood without knowing what a clitoris is, where it is and/or what to do with it. As someone who believes that all people have a fundamental right to knowledge about their own bodies, this is unjustifiable. Teaching about sex without teaching about pleasure is, in my opinion, damaging. But we also need to acknowledge that it is not equally damaging, and in fact reinforces old but alive ideas that sex is something men like and women endure.

In addition to being sexist, ignoring pleasure as a fundamental component of sex is heterosexist and can also be particularly damaging to men who have sex with men and women who have sex with women. Sex between women and between men is often discussed during sex education in terms of STD prevention. But here, once you remove pleasure from sex, it has no purpose. Non-heterosexual sex cannot result in procreation, so what's the point? This is the one thing that religious fundamentalists and abstinence-only educators are right about—when arguing that sex is not or should not be about pleasure, gay and lesbian sex does indeed seem rather odd and even wrong.

This thinking positions sex for pleasure as a waste of time rather than an activity that is itself often productive and important to those of all sexual orientations. Such limited education is invalidating to huge numbers of people and an erasure of their sexual desires and experiences. And the most-affected people are those who are not straight men.

Real Sex Education Breeds Smart Sexual Choices

Real sex education teaches that sexuality is natural and varied. And so, in teaching real sex education, we're also teaching teens to make smart sexual choices. When aware that there is sex beyond heterosexual intercourse, people can make better decisions about sexual gratification. They can choose masturbation, mutual masturbation, oral sex and a whole variety of other sexual acts—as non-abstinence alternatives with reduced risk of pregnancy or STDs, or just because many people find these acts enjoyable.

Knowing that sex is normal, healthy and not uniform also encourages people to learn what is most enjoyable for them and how to establish sexual boundaries. The social pressure to engage in certain kinds of sex acts as opposed to others (i.e. intercourse is largely valued more than outercourse) is far from healthy, and knowing this is vital. Once women, who are most likely to be taught otherwise, know that they are supposed to enjoy sex and might not enjoy certain kinds of sex, they also generally learn to start asking for what they want and feeling more confident in expressing what they don't. There's absolutely nothing to not like here.

Furthermore, studies show that sexual partners who discuss contraception are more likely to use it. This seems self-explanatory, but bears noting because it is often forgotten in arguments that sex education should be about safety and not pleasure. A person who feels guilt and discomfort over sex is generally going to have a difficult time talking about it. And what does that mean? It means no protection. If we want people to engage in safer sex, we need to give them the tools they need to engage in safer sex—and that's more than just showing them how to put on a condom.

Real Sex Education Is a Part of Anti-Rape Education

In order to teach about sexual assault intelligently and meaningfully, we have to teach about enthusiastic consent. We're still a far cry away from this point, but it should indeed be the goal. And I can't fathom how one might teach about enthusiastic consent without teaching about healthy sexuality as pleasurable.

I do not mean that men would never commit heterosexual rape if they knew and understood that women are supposed to enjoy sex too. In too many experiences, it wouldn't have made an ounce of difference. I doubt that my ex-boyfriend and rapist had ever heard the concept of enthusiastic consent in his life. Sex was for him, as it is for many, something to be obtained through coercion as opposed to something freely and happily negotiated. But I absolutely don't believe that if he had heard of enthusiastic consent, he wouldn't have inflicted sexual violence.

More simply than that, social perceptions of sex helped him to get away with it. Many men (and women!) don't understand what rape is. That doesn't mean that men who rape fail to understand when the woman has not fully and enthusiastically consented or when they're committing an act that is wrong—they simply fail or refuse to recognize that what they're doing actually falls under that scary word no one wants applied to them.

The goal is that enthusiastic consent models will help to change the thinking from "sex when someone says no and fights back is wrong" to "sex when someone doesn't openly and enthusiastically want it is wrong." Since all but maybe a tiny percentage of rapists realize that what they're doing is wrong (and the ones who don't are still responsible for their actions regardless), teaching enthusiastic consent will not stop rape on its own. I don't think that any one particular form of rape prevention education will. But I do strongly believe that rape is allowed to keep occurring because it is socially acceptable to the much larger group of people who aren't rapists but just "don't get what the big deal is" or believe it to be the victim's fault.

Specifically, real sex education is a necessary part of any good anti-rape education for those who are victims or potential victims. This is not because people are responsible for making sure they are not raped. But we do have a responsibility, particularly to young women, to give them the tools they need to recognize abuse.

Pleasure itself cannot be considered a benchmark for consent—automatic bodily reactions can cause physical, unwanted sexual arousal in a situation where there is not consent. On the opposite end of the spectrum, fully consensual sex can be dull. But the genuine desire for sexual pleasure and the expression of that desire should be an accepted standard.

The fact is, many abuse victims don't realize that they're being abused. They undergo the same trauma, and just don't understand why it hurts. I was never taught about enthusiastic consent. The phrase only entered my vocabulary a couple of years ago. It pains me to think of the difference that would have been made in my life if someone had taught me that I was supposed to want sexual contact and say so, otherwise it was wrong. Instead, I truly thought that consent included fearfully giving up after saying "no" twenty times. If taught differently, I don't know that I would have avoided the initial assaults. I do believe with all my heart that I would have gotten myself out of that situation sooner. At the time, I knew that rape and physical assault were inexcusable acts of violence generally committed against women. I just didn't realize that what was being done to me was rape. For that reason, it took me years to realize why I felt so traumatized.

Though I regret not getting out of that relationship, I don't blame myself. I know that only he was responsible for the violence, and that I did the best I could do at the time with what I had. But the fact remains that I could have done better if I had been given more.

Again, I don't think this kind of sex education, or any kind of sex education, is going to prevent all or even most rape. But don't we owe it to those for whom the information could someday be valuable? I believe that we do.

Real Sex Education Isn't Porn Education

Lastly, it's important to clarify that sex education which teaches about pleasure doesn't have to teach about technique (though elective college-level sex education that does this is great). Letting teens know that women usually achieve orgasm through rubbing of the clitoris, whether with fingers, mouth, object or penis, isn't the same as screening an instructional video on giving good cunnilingus. It's not the same as writing down the names of sex toy shops on the blackboard, or handing out diagrams of cool and exciting coital positions. And teaching that lubricant reduces pain and increases safety and pleasure during many kinds of sex should be thought of not as performance advice, but on par with vital lessons about condom use.

Real sex education is not the same as porn education. Instead, it's about teaching that pleasure is an important part of any sexual relationship. It's about teaching that there is nothing wrong with wanting to feel sexual pleasure and seeking it out, so long as it is done safely and responsibly. It's about teaching comfort with one's body, a lack of shame over desires, and that there is more to sex for all people than sticking penises inside of vaginas. Real sex education teaches how to go about making intelligent, safe choices, rather than just stating the choices available. I believe there is a big difference. And I believe that teaching teens to make smart choices about sex must involve teaching them that having sex, partnered or alone, can be a smart choice.

Periodical and Internet Sources Bibliography

The following articles have been selected to supplement the diverse views presented in this chapter.

Sandy Banks — "When Middle School Is Too Late for Sex Ed," *Los Angeles Times*, February 6, 2010.

Heather D. Boonstra — "Matter of Faith: Support for Comprehensive Sex Education Among Faith-Based Organizations," *Guttmacher Policy Review*, Winter 2008.

Kiki Bradley and Christine Kim — "The Case for Maintaining Abstinence Education Funding," Heritage Foundation WebMemo, no. 2562, July 24, 2009.

Conscience — "Are We Taking the Pleasure Out of Sex? What a Comprehensive Sexuality Education Program Should Look Like," March 2009.

Sarah Kliff — "The New Abstinence-Education Study Is Good News. So Why Are Liberals Freaking Out?" *Newsweek*, February 3, 2010.

Kathryn Jean Lopez — "The Hook-Up Is In," *National Review Online*, December 19, 2006. www.nationalreview.com.

Deborah Pan — "No Matter the Approach, Sex Ed Works," ABC News, December 19, 2007. http://abc.news.go.com

Amanda Paulson — "Abstinence-Only Study Could Alter Sex-Education Landscape," *Christian Science Monitor*, February 2, 2010.

Amy Sullivan — "How to Bring an End to the War Over Sex Ed," *Time*, March 19, 2009.

Steve Yoder — "Real Sex Ed Returns," *In These Times*, March 7, 2009.

OPPOSING
VIEWPOINTS®
SERIES

CHAPTER 3

How Can the Spread of Sexually Transmitted Diseases Be Reduced?

Chapter Preface

In April 1993, True Love Waits (TLW) was launched at the youth ministry national conference in Nashville, Tennessee. Sponsored by LifeWay Christian Resources, TLW advocates sexual purity, which it insists is more than abstaining from sex until marriage. "By Jesus' definition, being sexually pure means not even dwelling on thoughts of sex with someone other than a spouse," TLW states. "It means saying no to a physical relationship that causes you to be 'turned on' sexually. It means not looking at pornography or pictures that feed sexual thoughts." TLW also advises young people that sex is not a heat-of-the-moment decision and, therefore, can be avoided. "Sex is not an accident. Sex is progressive, meaning one act leads to another," it continues. "Things won't 'just happen' if you set boundaries and stick to them."

For those who pledge virginity, TLW offers several guarantees and advantages: total percent protection against sexually transmitted diseases (STDs) and pregnancy, avoidance of heartache and emotional distress, and better opportunities for success. For those who have engaged in premarital sexual activity, TLW proposes that an individual can reclaim his or her sexual purity. "When you decide you want to stay sexually pure from this day forward, then you can experience a second virginity," TLW explains. "This second virginity comes by asking for God's forgiveness through Jesus and by committing to stay sexually abstinent until marriage."

The first group of its kind, TLW has seen millions of pledgers across the globe signing "commitment cards" to not have sex until they marry. The Silver Ring Thing is another major virginity-pledge group, and elaborate "purity balls," or formal dances where daughters pledge to their fathers to remain virgins until marriage, are growing in popularity in the

United States. The authors in the following chapter deliberate upon the effectiveness of virginity pledges, condoms, and other means of STD prevention.

"The sad story is that kids who are trying to preserve their technical virginity are, in some cases, engaging in much riskier behavior."

Virginity Pledges Have No Impact on STD Rates Among Youths

Ceci Connolly

In the following viewpoint, Ceci Connolly proposes that adolescents who take virginity pledges are nearly as likely to be infected with a sexually transmitted disease (STD) as their non-pledging peers. A study shows that while those who pledge delay sexual debut, are less promiscuous, and marry younger, she contends that this group is less likely to use condoms, which can lead to an STD infection. In fact, Connolly suggests that promoting abstinence may lead young people to practice sexual behaviors more risky that vaginal sex. Connolly is a national staff writer for the Washington Post.

As you read, consider the following questions:

1. How does Connolly describe virginity pledges?

Ceci Connolly, "Teen Pledges Barely Cut STD Rates, Study Says," *Washington Post*, March 19, 2005. Reproduced by permission.

2. How does the author support her claim that teenagers who pledge are more likely to engage in riskier sexual behavior?

3. How do advocates defend virginity pledges, as stated by Connolly?

Teenagers who take virginity pledges—public declarations to abstain from sex—are almost as likely to be infected with a sexually transmitted disease as those who never made the pledge, an eight-year study released yesterday [March 18, 2005] found.

Although young people who sign a virginity pledge delay the initiation of sexual activity, marry at younger ages and have fewer sexual partners, they are also less likely to use condoms and more likely to experiment with oral and anal sex, said the researchers from Yale and Columbia universities.

"The sad story is that kids who are trying to preserve their technical virginity are, in some cases, engaging in much riskier behavior," said lead author Peter S. Bearman, a professor at Columbia's Institute for Social and Economic Research and Policy. "From a public health point of view, an abstinence movement that encourages no vaginal sex may inadvertently encourage other forms of alternative sex that are at higher risk of STDs."

Rates of Disease

The findings are based on the federally funded National Longitudinal Study of Adolescent Health, a survey begun in 1995 that tracked 20,000 young people from high school to young adulthood. At the start of the project, the students were 12 to 18 years old and agreed to detailed, sexually explicit interviews. They were re-interviewed in 1997 and again in 2002, when 11,500 also provided urine samples.

Virginity pledges emerged in the early 1990s based on the theory that young people would remain chaste if they had stronger community support—or pressure—to remain abstinent. Programs vary, but in most cases, teenagers voluntarily sign a pledge or publicly announce their intention to abstain from sex. Often pledgers receive a pin or ring to symbolize the promise and team up with an "accountability partner."

Since it was founded in 1993, the virginity group True Love Waits claims 2.4 million youths have signed a card stating: "Believing that true love waits, I make a commitment to God, myself, my family, those I date, and my future mate to be sexually pure until the day I enter marriage."

The study, published in the *Journal of Adolescent Health*, found that 20 percent of those surveyed said they had taken a virginity pledge. Bearman and co-author Hannah Brückner broke them into two categories—"inconsistent pledgers" and "consistent pledgers"—to reflect the fact that some changed their status or their responses between interviews. Among those youngsters, 61 percent of the consistent pledgers and 79 percent of the inconsistent pledgers reported having intercourse before marrying or prior to 2002 interviews.

Almost 7 percent of the students who did not make a pledge were diagnosed with an STD, compared with 6.4 percent of the "inconsistent pledgers" and 4.6 percent of the "consistent pledgers." Bearman said those differences were not "statistically significant," although Robert Rector, who studies domestic policy issues at the conservative Heritage [Foundation], said he interpreted the data to mean that young people committed to the abstinence pledge were less likely to become infected.

The study did not detect major geographic differences but found that minorities were far more likely to have an STD. About one quarter of African American girls in the survey tested positive for at least one STD in 2002.

In terms of high-risk behavior, the raw numbers were small, but the gap was statistically significant, Bearman said.

Just 2 percent of youth who never took a pledge said they had had anal or oral sex but not intercourse, compared with 13 percent of "consistent pledgers."

Debate on Abstinence

The report sparked an immediate, bitter debate over the wisdom of teaching premarital abstinence.

Deborah [M.] Roffman, an educator and author of *Sex and Sensibility: The Thinking Parent's Guide to Talking Sense About Sex*, said youths who take virginity pledges are often undereducated about sexual health. "Kids who are engaging in oral sex or anal sex will tell you they are practicing abstinence because they haven't had 'real sex' yet," she said.

Ralph DiClemente, a professor at Emory University's [Rollins] School of Public Health in Atlanta, compared virginity pledges to adults' efforts to make New Year's resolutions.

"I wish it was that easy. We'd all be a lot healthier," he said. "If we can't do it as adults, why would we expect kids to be able to handle those issues?"

But Joe S. McIlhaney Jr., chairman of the Medical Institute for Sexual Health, said the study offers an incomplete picture because it could not say whether sexually active teens who did not take a pledge had been pregnant or treated for an STD before the 2002 testing. The analysis "doesn't prove or disprove" assertions that virginity pledges are flawed, he said.

On the other hand, Bill Smith, public policy vice president for the Sexuality Information and Education Council of the United States, said, "Not only do virginity pledges not work to keep our young people safe, they are causing harm by undermining condom use, contraception and medical treatment."

Conservative academics said the paper overlooked earlier important findings about adolescents who take virginity pledges, most notably that they have fewer pregnancies and out-of-wedlock births.

"It's hugely successful on those variables," Rector said. "Bearman has focused in on the one variable he thinks can show they [pledgers] don't do better."

President [George W.] Bush has requested $206 million in federal funding for abstinence-only programs this year [in 2005].

Several True Love Waits officials were unavailable Friday, according to a receptionist. Telephone calls to another virginity group, the Silver Ring Thing, were not returned.

| "Overall, virginity pledge programs have
a strong record of success."

Virginity Pledges Reduce STD Rates Among Youths

Robert Rector and Kirk Johnson

Robert Rector is senior research fellow at the Heritage Foundation, where Kirk Johnson is senior policy analyst in the Center for Data Analysis. In the following viewpoint, Rector and Johnson rebuke allegations that adolescents who take virginity pledges have the same rates of sexually transmitted disease (STD) infections as those who do not. The authors argue that researchers behind the claims focused on a tiny subgroup of pledgers who engaged in sexual behaviors riskier than vaginal intercourse. Moreover, they say that the lower incidences of STDs among pledgers are indeed statistically significant—pledgers are 25 percent less likely to contract an STD. The researchers' findings, Rector and Johnson conclude, are based on skewed and incomplete evidence.

As you read, consider the following questions:

1. What do the researchers against virginity pledges not state, according to the authors?

Robert Rector and Kirk Johnson, "Virginity Pledgers Have Lower STD Rates and Engage in Fewer Risky Sexual Behaviors," Heritage Foundation WebMemo #762, June 14, 2005. Reproduced by permission.

2. What figures do Rector and Johnson cite to claim that the high-risk group of pledgers is miniscule?

3. How do Rector and Johnson respond to the claim that pledgers are less likely to use condoms?

For more than a decade, organizations such as True Love Waits have encouraged young people to abstain from sexual activity. As part of these programs, young people are encouraged to take a verbal or written pledge to abstain from sex until marriage.

An article by professors Peter [S.] Bearman and Hannah Brückner in the April 2005 issue of the *Journal of Adolescent Health* strongly attacked virginity pledge programs and abstinence education in general. The article stated that youth who took virginity pledges had the same sexually transmitted disease (STD) rates as non-pledgers. It also strongly suggested that virginity pledgers were more likely to engage in unhealthy anal and oral sex. The report garnered widespread media attention across the nation. A reexamination of the data, however, reveals that Bearman and Brückner's conclusions were inaccurate. Moreover, in crucial respects they misled the press and public.

Bearman and Brückner tested the long-term effects of virginity pledge programs, examining the health and risk behaviors of young adults (with an average age of 22) who had taken a virginity pledge as adolescents. Their analysis was based on the National Longitudinal Study of Adolescent Health ("Add Health"), a database funded by the federal government. We used this same database to reexamine the issues they raised.

Several discrepancies were immediately apparent. For starters, the Add Health data clearly reveal that virginity pledgers are less likely to engage in oral or anal sex when compared to non-pledgers. In addition, virginity pledgers who have become sexually active (engaged in vaginal, oral, or anal sex) are still

A Constant Reminder

Make plans well in advance so parents can select a ring or some other symbol to be used in this ceremony. You may choose to use candles in order to make the experience even more visually memorable to the church. If you choose to use candles, refer to them as a symbol of the commitment made in a dark world filled with unknown dangers and life-threatening consequences. Like the candle, their commitment will generate light, which will make the path clear for others to follow in their footsteps.

Our lives are filled with milestones and remembrances. They remind us of where we have been and where we are going. In the truest sense they give us a reminder of the course that is ahead. Temptation lurks in every corner for youth. A ring as a constant visual reminder of this commitment will reinforce the commitment and remind us of whom we are in Christ and the path that is set before us.

True Love Waits,
"Ring Ceremony for True Love Waits,"
Sample Order of Worship for True Love Waits,
www.lifeway.com.

less likely to engage in oral or anal sex when compared to sexually active non-pledgers. This lower level of risk behavior puts virginity pledgers at lower risk for sexually transmitted diseases relative to non-pledgers.

Concluding the Opposite

How do Bearman and Brückner conclude the opposite? In a narrow sense, they do not. Although they strongly suggest that pledgers are more likely to engage in anal and oral sex, they never actually state that. In fact, they very carefully avoid making any clear statements about the sexual risk behaviors of pledgers and non-pledgers as a whole. Instead, they have culled through the Add Health sample looking for tiny subgroups of pledgers with higher risk behaviors. They then describe the risk behaviors of these tiny groups and let the press infer that they are talking about pledgers in general.

The centerpiece of their argument about pledgers and heightened sexual risk activity is a small group of pledgers who engaged in anal sex without vaginal sex. This "risk group" consists of 21 persons out of a sample of 14,116. Bearman and Brückner focus on this microscopic group while failing to inform their audience of the obvious and critical fact that pledgers as a whole are substantially less likely to engage in anal sex when compared to non-pledgers.

This tactic is akin to finding a small rocky island in the middle of the ocean, describing the island in detail without describing the surrounding ocean, and then suggesting that the ocean is dry and rocky. It is junk science.

With regard to STDs, Bearman and Brückner actually found that adolescents who made virginity pledges were less likely to have STDs as young adults than were non-pledgers, but concluded that this difference was not statistically significant. This conclusion was based on limitations in their methodology. In fact, the same methods that they used to demonstrate that virginity pledges do not reduce STDs also demonstrate that condom use does not reduce STDs.

One problem is that Bearman and Brückner examined only one of several STD measures available in the Add Health data file. Analysis of the remaining measures reveals that adolescent virginity pledging is strongly associated with reduced STDs among young adults. These results are statistically significant in four of the five STD measures examined and are very near significance on the fifth measure. With all the STD measures, the allegedly ineffective virginity pledge is actually a better predictor of STD reduction than is condom use. On average, individuals who took virginity pledges as adolescents were 25 percent less likely to have STDs as young adults than non-pledgers from identical socioeconomic backgrounds.

Further, Bearman and Brückner's suggestion that virginity pledgers are ignorant about contraception is also inaccurate. Although virginity pledgers were less likely to use contraception at the very first occurrence of intercourse, differences in contraceptive use between pledgers and non-pledgers disappear quickly. In young adult years, sexually active pledgers are as likely to use contraception as non-pledgers.

An Array of Positive Outcomes

Of course, virginity pledge programs are not omnipotent. Many years will pass between the time an adolescent takes a pledge and the time he or she reaches adulthood. These years will be full of events and forces that either reinforce or, more likely, undermine the youth's commitment to abstinence. Despite these forces, taking a virginity pledge is associated with a broad array of positive outcomes. Although most pledgers fall short of their goal of abstaining until marriage, in general, they still do a lot better in life. Compared to non-pledgers from the same social backgrounds, pledgers have far fewer sex partners. Pledgers are also less likely to engage in sex while in high school, less likely to experience teen pregnancy, less likely to have a child out of wedlock, less likely to have children in their teen and young adult years, and less likely to engage in non-marital sex as young adults.

Overall, virginity pledge programs have a strong record of success. They are among the few institutions in society teaching self-restraint to youth awash in a culture of narcissism and sexual permissiveness. They have been unfairly maligned by two academics who should know better.

"Condoms remain an important tool in our ongoing efforts to achieve sexual and reproductive health."

Condoms Protect Against STDs

Judith Reichman

Judith Reichman is a gynecologist and women's health contributor for NBC's Today. *In the following viewpoint, the author asserts that condoms can effectively protect against various sexually transmitted diseases (STDs). Medical studies consistently demonstrate that condoms—even when used inconsistently or sometimes improperly—significantly cut the infection rates of HIV and human papillomavirus (HPV) and are known to protect from gonorrhea, chlamydia, and herpes, she insists. And while the HPV vaccination offers some hope in reducing the incidences of cervical cancers, Reichman contends that condoms still play a role in preventing STDs.*

As you read, consider the following questions:

1. What is "typical use" failure of condoms, as stated by the author?

Judith Reichman, "Do Condoms Really Protect Against STDs?" Today.msnbc.msn.com, August 2, 2006. Reproduced by permission.

2. How does the author address the claim that promoting condom use increases promiscuity?

3. According to Reichman, why doesn't the HPV vaccine make condoms less important?

Condoms have a fascinating history. In 1000 B.C., Egyptian men used a linen sheath for protection against disease. By the 1700s, condoms were made from animal intestines and described as "a cobweb against infection." In the 1800s, rubber became the condom material of choice. Natural rubber latex was introduced in the early 1900s, and by the 1950s, lubricated condoms were widely marketed. Since then, we have seen the advent of polyurethane condoms. Currently, condoms have become thinner and stronger, and they come in various sizes, shapes, colors and, yes, even flavors. Clearly, we've come a long way from using Egyptian linen penis wraps for disease protection. But do modern condoms prevent the transmission of STDs [sexually transmitted diseases]? Here are a few common questions about them and the latest information on them.

Condom Use and STDs

Do condoms reduce the risk of STDs, including HIV [human immunodeficiency virus]? Not always. Even though it makes sense that preventing direct skin-to-skin (or vaginal mucosa) contact during intercourse would prevent viruses, bacteria and sperm from passing between partners, warnings about condom effectiveness prevail. Condoms are certainly not foolproof when it comes to contraception. If 100 women and their partners use condoms for a year in what is described as "perfect use," two will become pregnant. With "typical use" (not used consistently or correctly) 15 women will become pregnant. This "typical use" failure rate is rarely due to a faulty condom, but rather to faulty application or no application. (Note, condoms in the U.S. are electronically tested for holes and defects and serial lots are tested for strength.)

When it comes to STD information and labeling, condoms have come under social, religious, political and medical scrutiny. Absolute standards for STD protection have been strongly advocated and, of course, are correct: *The best way to ensure 100 percent protection against STDs is for both partners to abstain from sexual intercourse until marriage and then to refrain from extramarital sex.* But as we know, this has not been applicable or practical for many (if not a majority) of individuals both in the U.S. and the developing world. In 2001, a law was passed that required the Food and Drug Administration [FDA] to reexamine condom labels to determine the "medical accuracy" of their description of condoms' effectiveness in preventing human papillomavirus (HPV) infections as well as other STDs. Since then, there has subsequently been considerable effort to pressure the FDA to add a warning to condoms about their lack of protection.

But in the past six years, further studies have supplied evidence that should set the condom issue straight. Medical evidence now shows that consistent use of condoms reduces the risk of transmission in men and women of

- HIV (by 80 percent)

- Gonorrhea

- Chlamydia

- Herpes simplex virus

(Note: The prevention of the last three STDs has not been absolutely quantified, because no one is suggesting that a person known to have one of these treatable infections have regular intercourse with an unaffected partner, unless they use condoms and/or are appropriately treated. Condom protection against HIV has been studied, especially in countries where therapies are often unavailable or unaffordable.)

We now have a new study published in the *New England Journal of Medicine* that convincingly demonstrates that condom use also reduces the risk of HPV infection in women.

A Significant HPV Study

What was novel or important about this HPV study? HPV transmission is extraordinarily common. Genital HPV has now been shown to occur at some point in up to 80 percent of sexually active young women within five years of becoming sexually active. If the virus is not killed by a woman's immune system (which is what usually happens), it goes on to cause pre-cancers and cancers in the cervix, vagina, vulva skin and anus, as well as benign but physically disturbing warts.

This three-year study followed 82 female university students who had previously never had intercourse with a male partner. For three years, they answered simple questions on their computer every two weeks about their sexual behavior (whether they used condoms, how often they had intercourse, whether their partners had had previous partners, and if there was skin-to-skin contact without condom use). They were also tested every four months for HPV and had a Pap test. The women whose partners always wore a condom during sex were 70 percent less likely to become infected with HPV than those whose partners used protection less than 5 percent of the time. And even women whose partners used condoms just more than half of the time had a 50 percent reduction in their development of HPV.

None of the women whose partners always used condoms developed pre-cancerous lesions (called cervical squamous intraepithelial lesions) during the three-year period. But 14 women whose partners did not use condoms or used them inconsistently developed these lesions, which were detected on their Pap smears. The FDA is currently revising rules for claims that manufacturers can make on how well condoms prevent STDs and HPV, and this study may influence their final recommendations.

More Sex or Safer Sex?

Does promoting condom use lead to an increase in promiscuous sex? Let me first point out that according to data published by the Guttmacher Institute (as well as the Youth Risk [Behavior] Surveillance survey of 2003), over 50 percent of high school girls have begun having intercourse between the ages of 15 and 18. The institute has also published well-accepted data that shows that contraceptive education does not encourage sexual activity. Of interest is the fact that only 15 percent of Americans want abstinence-only education taught in classrooms, but four in 10 sex education teachers don't teach about contraceptive methods or teach that it is ineffective. We still have the highest rate of teen pregnancy in the developed world! Lack of contraceptive education is certainly not helping.

Moreover, analysis on the use of condoms to reduce the risk of HIV in 174 studies (with over 100,000 participants) did not show that condom use increased unsafe sexual behavior. Most major health institutions now support an ABC approach for prevention of HIV and other STDs. ABC stands for

- Abstinence

- Be Faithful

- Use Condoms

For those who choose to be sexually active, there is medically sound reassurance that condom use can reduce the risk of STDs, but only when used consistently and correctly. Condoms, the "c" in this all-important acronym, can help attain *safer sex*.

The HPV Vaccine and Condom Use

Will the new HPV vaccine make condom use less important? No. The vaccine that was recently approved by the FDA for HPV and cervical cancer protection (Gardasil, manufactured by Merck & Co.) specifically targets four types of HPV viruses, which cause 70 percent of cervical cancers and 90 percent of genital warts as well as pre-cancerous lesions of the cervix and vagina. This vaccine is effective in preventing cancers and active infections from these four types of HPV in women who have not yet been infected. It doesn't protect those who have already been infected with these viruses. Gardasil is therefore slated for use in adolescent girls and young women between the ages of 9 and 26. The vaccine is given through three injections over a course of six months. Each shot costs $120. Within one month of finishing the last injection, immunity is present. In essence, this is a "before you have sex" or "before you are infected" vaccine. It will probably be given (like the hepatitis vaccine) by pediatricians or by gynecologists who see adolescent girls and young women.

(Note: The new recommendation by the American College of Obstetricians and Gynecologists is that 13- to 15-year-old girls have an initial ob-gyn visit to discuss their development, periods and future reproductive health issues. A pelvic exam is not felt to be necessary at this time ... *but it certainly would be an appropriate time to discuss and provide immunization.*)

Clearly a lot of issues need to be resolved about this new vaccine. How long is it protective? (So far data has shown efficacy continues for at least five years.) Will booster shots be necessary? Who will pay? Should we immunize young women who have already had sex but whose previous HPV status is unknown? And let's not forget that as good as this vaccine may be in preventing cervical cancer, there are other types of HPV infections that can potentially cause cancer. The vaccine will not protect against all the other STDs and, of course, is not a contraceptive.

Condoms remain an important tool in our ongoing efforts to achieve sexual and reproductive health. We now have additional evidence that when it comes to the horrifically prevalent and transmittable HPV, condom protection is effective.

> "With Viagra and Internet dating sites
> at their fingertips, a growing number
> of seniors are enjoying a renaissance
> between the sheets, but some are pay-
> ing the piper, contracting sexually
> transmitted diseases."

Senior Citizens Should Use Condoms to Prevent STDs

Deborah Kotz

In the following viewpoint, Deborah Kotz warns that older Americans chance being infected with sexually transmitted diseases (STDs) and should always use condoms. This group is at risk, Kotz writes, because pregnancy is no longer a factor, and physicians do not address their senior patients' sexual behaviors. Moreover, postmenopausal women are especially vulnerable to blood-borne infections such as HIV and chlamydia and may also contract genital warts, adds the author. Covering women's issues and psychology, Kotz is a senior writer in the Health section at U.S. News & World Report.

Deborah Kotz, "Sex Ed for Seniors: You Still Need Those Condoms," *U.S. News & World Report*, August 13, 2007. Reproduced by permission.

As you read, consider the following questions:

1. What statistics does the author cite about seniors and condom use?

2. Why are postmenopausal women at special risk of blood-borne infections, according to Kotz?

3. How did New York City and southern Florida increase awareness of condoms and HIV among seniors, as described by Kotz?

When Jane Fowler hit the dating scene after her 23-year marriage ended in divorce, she didn't think she needed to use protection when she had sex. "I wasn't worried about getting pregnant," says the 72-year-old retired journalist from Kansas City, Mo., "and the man I was seeing was an old friend, also recently divorced." So she was shocked to learn, after having a routine blood test in 1991, that she'd been infected with HIV [human immunodeficiency virus], a nightmare she hopes to help others avoid by lecturing at senior health fairs. "My mantra is that you never know the sexual history of anyone but yourself."

With Viagra and Internet dating sites at their fingertips, a growing number of seniors are enjoying a renaissance between the sheets, but some are paying the piper, contracting sexually transmitted diseases. As HIV carriers live longer, the majority will be over age 50 by 2015, and even now about 15 percent of new infections occur in this age group, according to the Centers for Disease Control and Prevention [CDC]. Other STDs [sexually transmitted diseases], including herpes, chlamydia, and human papillomavirus, which is linked to cervical cancer, are also making the rounds. "While it's a good thing that older people are more sexually active, they need to connect the dots, see that they're at increased risk, and make sure they use condoms," says Anthony Fauci, director of the National Institute of Allergy and Infectious Diseases.

Fewer Tested, Often Misdiagnosed

Few older adults get tested for HIV, leading to late-stage diagnoses that raise the potential to spread the virus unknowingly. Since common symptoms of HIV, such as fatigue, weight loss, and sleeplessness, also increase with age, the virus is often misdiagnosed among older adults, allowing it to spread.

Julie Zeveloff,
"Condoms for Seniors: Gearing Up for the Graying of AIDS,"
Columbia News Service, April 1, 2008.

Unsafe at Any Age

But many folks haven't gotten the message. In a small survey conducted by University of Chicago researchers, nearly 60 percent of unmarried women ages 58 to 93 said they didn't use a condom the last time they had sex. Even more disturbing, an Ohio University study found that about 27 percent of HIV-infected men and 35 percent of HIV-infected women over 50 sometimes have sex without using condoms.

Researchers believe doctors, unwilling to broach the topic of STDs, may be partly to blame. The University of Chicago survey found that nearly half of the respondents didn't talk to their doctors about their sex life. "Older women think doctors should ask them about it but won't initiate the discussion themselves," says study author Stacy Lindau. Doctors may also misdiagnose early symptoms of HIV infection—fatigue, weakness, memory changes—as normal signs of aging. "I've seen HIV patients in their late 50s and early 60s who tell me they had gone to their doctors several times over many months before they were finally tested for HIV," says psychologist Timothy Heckman, who coauthored the Ohio University study.

Raising Awareness

New HIV screening recommendations issued by the CDC last September [in 2006] may mitigate the problem. The agency urged doctors to do voluntary blood tests in all patients ages 13 to 64 in order to prevent the 50 to 70 percent of new infections spread by those who are unaware they have the virus. It says screening isn't cost effective in those over 65 because they cause just 2 percent of new infections. But Heckman, who doesn't think there should be an age limit, points out that the CDC's own data show higher death rates in older adults diagnosed with full-blown AIDS possibly because of complicating problems like diabetes, heart disease, or an aging immune system.

Postmenopausal women, moreover, may be particularly prone to getting infected with blood-borne diseases like HIV or chlamydia in the first place. That's because their thinner and more fragile vaginal lining can easily tear during penetration, allowing pathogens to enter the bloodstream. And new research indicates that older women are at risk of getting infected with HPV [human papillomavirus], which can give rise to genital warts or cervical cancer. "We once thought that they were just getting a reactivation of an old infection, but now we think these might be new infections from unprotected sex," says Lindau, who is actively researching this subject.

The most effective way to prevent disease is to use condoms consistently. Research indicates they're nearly 90 percent effective against HIV transmission. And a 2006 *New England Journal of Medicine* study found that women whose partners used condoms all the time were 70 percent less likely to acquire HPV than those whose partners rarely used them. The female condom is also an effective barrier, says Lindau.

Perhaps the most important first step, public health officials believe, is simply making seniors aware of the risks. Several weeks ago, New York City officials began handing out educational materials and condoms at more than 320 senior centers, while urging all older New Yorkers to get tested for HIV as part of their regular checkups. Southern Florida's Senior HIV Intervention Project distributes prophylactics and safe-sex advice at Jewish community centers, assisted-living facilities, and bereavement group meetings. Program volunteer Miriam Schuler, an 88-year-old great-grandmother from Tamarac, Fla., often finds a little humor helps to wash down the warnings. "If a man comes up and sees the condoms, I tell him, 'Put one in your pocket; make your friends jealous!'" she says. "For women, I tell them to put some condoms in a dish on their coffee table as a conversation piece."

> *"There are instances in which condom use alone—or the use of dental dams and gloves—cannot offer the same level of protection they can in other instances."*

Condoms Do Not Protect Fully Against Some STDs

Heather Corinna

Heather Corinna is the founder of Scarleteen, a teen website about sexual health and issues. In the following viewpoint, Corinna advises that condoms do not provide total protection against sexually transmitted diseases (STDs) spread through skin-to-skin contact, such as human papillomavirus (HPV), genital warts, and herpes. Condoms do not completely cover the genital area, and sores and warts are not always visible or obvious, she explains. Corinna, however, does not recommend abstinence if it impacts the quality of life, reiterating that individuals should be aware of the risks when considering safer sex practices.

As you read, consider the following questions:

1. What areas do condoms only protect, according to Corinna?

Heather Corinna, "HPV & Herpes: Why Safer Sex Isn't Always Safe Enough," Scarleteen, July 2010. Reproduced by permission.

2. How does Corinna describe the scope of the HPV problem in the United States?

3. What characterizes a sexual partner that puts one greatly at risk of STDs, as stated by Corinna?

At some point, you have probably heard someone—perhaps even a school or community or health group—say that condoms are not effective when it comes to safer sex and preventing the spread of sexually transmitted disease and infection. Unfortunately, some myths are propagated about condom use in this way.

You might hear someone say that latex condoms have "holes" in them which are small enough to let disease, infection or semen through. This is very much not so. You may have heard someone say that condoms aren't at all effective because they break all of the time. This is also not often the case. In fact, when used correctly, and for ALL genital and/or oral contact, it's actually quite rare for condoms to break.

However, myths and misinformation aside, there are instances in which condom use alone—or the use of dental dams and gloves—cannot offer the same level of protection they can in other instances, with STIs [sexually transmitted infections] which are transmitted not via fluid exchange, but by skin-to-skin contact, namely two of the most common STIs, HPV [human papillomavirus] and herpes.

A condom does not cover the entire genital area, and these infections can be transmitted via sores or warts (which may or may not always be visible or readily apparent) and by contact with parts of the genitals NOT covered by the condom (in other words, the genital anatomy besides the penile shaft and vaginal canal). Condom use for vaginal, oral or anal sex and dental dam use for anal/oral play or female oral sex certainly DOES make a difference—around 70% of one, which is a whole lot better than 0%—and cut the chances of transmitting or contracting those infections (and others for which condoms and latex barriers are greatly effective). But it's important to realize that in the cases of infections like HPV and herpes, safer sex tools and practices cannot provide complete protection.

In other words, even when using condoms, dams or gloves, you may still be at a considerable risk of transmitting or contracting HPV (human papillomavirus, some strains of which cause genital warts) or HSV-2 (genital herpes).

HPV Is Among Most Common STIs

HPV is one of the most common STIs among young, sexually active people under 22. At any one time, an estimated 20 million people in the United States have genital HPV infections that can be transmitted to others. Every year, about 6 million people acquire a genital HPV infection. A recent U.S. study among female college students found that an average of 14 percent became infected with genital HPV each year. About 43 percent of the women in the study were infected with HPV during the three-year study period. Typical prevalence of HPV for women under the age of 25 is between 28 and 46 percent of all women.

Most estimates suggest that one out of every three sexually active young adults may carry HPV, yet far fewer have visible, active warts they could recognize or self-diagnose (as little as only 1–2%), though they are infected and CAN and likely will still transmit HPV. Some strains of HPV may cause cervical cancer and make a person with the infection more susceptible to other infectious diseases, like HIV. It is not yet curable. Some people may shed or suppress the virus, but there is no accurate way of knowing who has and who has not at this time. . . .

The Spread of Herpes

HSV-2—genital herpes—is one of the most common sexually transmitted diseases in the United States, with as many as one million people in the United States becoming infected each year. While genital herpes continues to spread across all social, economic, racial and ethnic boundaries, prevalence of infection increased most dramatically in teens and young adults in the late 1980s and early 1990s. In a national household survey, less than 10 percent of people who tested positive with herpes knew they were infected. 45 million people are infected with genital herpes, about one in every five people has it. In addition, HSV-1 (oral herpes/cold sores) is carried by about one in two people in the United States (that's at least 50%), and can be spread via oral or oral/genital contact, creating a genital herpes infection with HSV-1. Like HPV, there is currently no cure for herpes infections. . . .

This does NOT mean the smart thing to do is to say, "Then why bother with safer sex?" and not practice at all, because there are both other diseases and infections out there they DO offer protection from, and use still DOES greatly decrease your risk (by 50% at a minimum) of contracting HPV and herpes as well.

We don't say these things to scare you, but rather so that you can just make informed choices based on what level of risk feels manageable to you.

And the truth right now in time is that should you choose to engage in manual . . . , oral . . . , vaginal or anal sex right now, even when you do so safely (with safer sex practices and regular testing for you and your partner, and by limiting the number of partners), you are taking a decent risk of contracting HPV or herpes simplex. While both of these infections can be treated—and thus, you can reduce or decrease your symptoms—they cannot be cured. So, while one can feel just fine with either infection in many cases with certain treatments and medications, the infection itself may not go away and may remain transmissible to all the sexual partners of an infected person (and in the case of oral herpes, can also be, and is, transmitted by nonsexual contact as well) for the whole

Condom Failure

Condom failure may or may not result in pregnancy or disease transmission. Condom failure refers only to what happens to the device, not to the consequences of the failure.

Condom breakage can be in the form of a burst, rip or tear, which may occur at the tip, along the shaft or near the opening of the condom. Breakage can occur while opening the condom package, putting the condom on the penis, during intercourse, withdrawing the penis, or removing the condom.

Slippage may be partial or complete. During partial slippage, part or all of the condom slips down the shaft of the penis. Partial slippage can also happen in the form of tip displacement, in which case the closed end of the condom is no longer held tightly around the end of the penis. For complete slippage to occur, the condom must become separated from the penis. Slippage can occur during intercourse or withdrawal.

Alan B. Spruyt, "Defining 'Condom Failure,'"
The Latex Condom: Recent Advances, Future Directions.
Eds. Erin T. McNeill et al. Family Health International, 1998.
www.fhi.org.

of their life. If you know you or a partner have either of these infections, even with safer sex, you have a risk of contracting or transmitting them.

Further Complications

HPV and herpes infections become further complicated by the fact that there are presently not good tests or screenings which can be done to discover either accurately in many cases, unless there are active sores or warts which are visible. Such is the case in terms of HPV, where there often are not visible symptoms, especially in men (and there currently is no approved HPV test for men: in other words, a man cannot currently be tested for HPV), and in women as well—or unless an infection has created other symptoms or complications in the body.

What's the answer? There isn't an easy one. In most cases, if you simply chose to abstain from all sexual activities, forever, you could likely avoid HPV and HSV-2. But very few people are going to do that, and we do have to consider in making sexual choices how they will impact our quality of life. Cutting off sexual or affectionate contact with all people, or with sexual partners within reasonable limits (those of their and our own physical, emotional safety and health, in general) for all of our lives would, for many of us, greatly impact and reduce our quality of life, potentially more than an infection would. But to make informed choices, we should consider that even with safer sex practices in play—even with only one sexual partner—we may still be taking a substantial risk at contracting or transmitting skin-to-skin STDs and STIs.

Steps to Safety

If you're going to be sexually active knowing and accepting that, then there are some steps you can take to help heighten your safety levels.

- If you're a young woman under the age of 26, even if you've already become sexually active, you can talk to your doctor about and consider getting the HPV vaccine, which can offer protection from four common strains of HPV.

- Practice safer sex, especially for oral, vaginal and manual sex. Practicing safer sex protects you greatly from all STDs and STIs, and even in terms of HPV and herpes, using condoms and other latex barriers does decrease your risk substantially.

- Read up on skin-to-skin STDs and STIs to find out what noticeable symptoms might be when they are present, and have yourself and your partner(s) be on the lookout for those symptoms, primarily: warts, which often are small, whitish or pinkish, and raised with a cauliflower-like texture, and herpes zoster sores, which look a bit like red, raw blisters, or may crust over slightly on the top. In addition, at the sign of any unusual itching burning or tingling of the genitals, check in with your doctor. As well, don't accept that a lack of symptoms or partners for intercourse means you or your partner are not carrying any STDs or STIs—that is simply not intelligent. Instead, have annual or biannual sexual health visits at your local clinic, or with your OB/GYN and get full STD and STI screens, without fail, at least every year.

- Reduce the number of sexual partners you have. This is not a ploy to say everyone needs to be or should be monogamous. However, if you are with sexual partners who you cannot trust, do not know well over time, and with whom you cannot both check in on your sexual health together and with your doctors openly and regularly, you are greatly increasing your risks. Math alone is enough to tell us that keeping track of all of those things between two or three people just over one year can be a serious challenge—trying to do it for real with more can be difficult if not impossible for most people.

- Don't let ignorance or denial drive your car. Thinking you and yours can't have HPV, herpes or any other infection doesn't offer any protection, and it can't make existing infections, or the likelihood of transmitting them, go away. Sizing up your risk factors for these things is a Big Life Decision. You wouldn't blow off similar life choices that could impact the rest of your life, like finishing high school, or becoming pregnant, so be just as wise here; take the time to give these things thought, and really weigh your options, needs and wants. It's your choice, but only if you actively make it.

| "Strong STD prevention, testing, and treatment can play a vital role in comprehensive programs to prevent sexual transmission of HIV."

Routine STD Testing and Treatment Can Reduce the Spread of HIV

Centers for Disease Control and Prevention

Testing and treating sexually transmitted diseases (STDs) can help prevent the spread of HIV, the Centers for Disease Control and Prevention (CDC) states in the following viewpoint. For example, genital ulcers from herpes or syphilis increase the susceptibility of contracting HIV, the CDC says. Furthermore, the CDC claims that HIV-positive individuals infected with STDs are more likely to shed HIV in their genital secretions, increasing the risk of transmitting the virus to their partners. Therefore, the CDC recommends comprehensive programs that include prevention, testing, and treatment. Formed in 1992, the CDC is a federal agency under the US Department of Health and Human Services.

As you read, consider the following questions:

1. How does gonorrhea affect men who have HIV, as described by the CDC?

2. How can tracking STD trends play a role in the HIV epidemic, in the CDC's view?

3. What does the CDC recommend for people diagnosed with or suspected to have an STD?

Testing and treatment of sexually transmitted diseases (STDs) can be an effective tool in preventing the spread of HIV [human immunodeficiency virus], the virus that causes AIDS [acquired immune deficiency syndrome]. An understanding of the relationship between STDs and HIV infection can help in the development of effective HIV prevention programs for persons with high-risk sexual behaviors.

The Link Between STDs and HIV Infection

Individuals who are infected with STDs are at least two to five times more likely than uninfected individuals to acquire HIV infection if they are exposed to the virus through sexual contact. In addition, if an HIV-infected individual is also infected with another STD, that person is more likely to transmit HIV through sexual contact than other HIV-infected persons.

There is substantial biological evidence demonstrating that the presence of other STDs increases the likelihood of both transmitting and acquiring HIV.

- Increased susceptibility. STDs appear to increase susceptibility to HIV infection by two mechanisms. Genital ulcers (e.g., syphilis, herpes, or chancroid) result in breaks in the genital tract lining or skin. These breaks create a portal of entry for HIV. Additionally, inflammation resulting from genital ulcers or non-ulcerative STDs (e.g., chlamydia, gonorrhea, and trichomoniasis) increase the concentration of cells in genital secretions that can serve as targets for HIV (e.g., CD4+ cells).

- Increased infectiousness. STDs also appear to increase the risk of an HIV-infected person transmitting the virus to his or her sex partners. Studies have shown that HIV-infected individuals who are also infected with other STDs are particularly likely to shed HIV in their genital secretions. For example, men who are infected with both gonorrhea and HIV are more than twice as likely to have HIV in their genital secretions than are those who are infected only with HIV. Moreover, the median concentration of HIV in semen is as much as 10 times higher in men who are infected with both gonorrhea and HIV than in men infected only with HIV. The higher the concentration of HIV in semen or genital fluids, the more likely it is that HIV will be transmitted to a sex partner.

STD Treatment Slows the Spread of HIV Infection

Evidence from intervention studies indicates that detecting and treating STDs may reduce HIV transmission.

- STD treatment reduces an individual's ability to transmit HIV. Studies have shown that treating STDs in HIV-infected individuals decreases both the amount of HIV in genital secretions and how frequently HIV is found in those secretions.

- Herpes can make people more susceptible to HIV infection, and it can make HIV-infected individuals more infectious. It is critical that all individuals, especially those with herpes, know whether they are infected with HIV and, if uninfected with HIV, take measures to protect themselves from infection with HIV.

- Among individuals with both herpes and HIV, trials are under way studying if treatment of genital herpes helps prevent HIV transmission to partners.

The Implications for HIV Prevention

Strong STD prevention, testing, and treatment can play a vital role in comprehensive programs to prevent sexual transmission of HIV. Furthermore, STD trends can offer important insights into where the HIV epidemic may grow, making STD surveillance data helpful in forecasting where HIV rates are likely to increase. Better linkages are needed between HIV and STD prevention efforts nationwide in order to control both epidemics.

In the context of persistently high prevalence of STDs in many parts of the United States and with emerging evidence that the U.S. HIV epidemic increasingly is affecting populations with the highest rates of curable STDs, the CDC [Centers for Disease Control and Prevention]/HRSA [Human Resources and Services Administration] Advisory Committee on HIV/AIDS and STD Prevention and Treatment (CHAC [HSPT]) recommended the following:

- Early detection and treatment of curable STDs should become a major, explicit component of comprehensive HIV prevention programs at national, state, and local levels.

- In areas where STDs that facilitate HIV transmission are prevalent, screening and treatment programs should be expanded.

- HIV testing should always be recommended for individuals who are diagnosed with or suspected to have an STD.

- HIV and STD prevention programs in the United States, together with private and public sector partners, should take joint responsibility for implementing these strategies.

CHAC[HSPT] also notes that early detection and treatment of STDs should be only one component of a comprehensive HIV prevention program, which also must include a range of social, behavioral, and biomedical interventions.

Periodical and Internet Sources Bibliography

The following articles have been selected to supplement the diverse views presented in this chapter.

Associated Press	"For Condoms, Maybe Size Matters After All," October 11, 2007.
Neela Banerjee	"Dancing the Night Away, with a Higher Purpose," *New York Times*, May 19, 2008.
CBS News	"The Female Condom: Effective, Underused," February 11, 2010. www.cbsnews.com.
Helen Cordes	"Take Your Politics to Bed: After Half a Century of the Pill, It's Time to Pass the Birth Control Baton to Men," *Herizons*, April 2010.
Sherri Day	"Virginity Pledges Under Scrutiny," *St. Petersburg Times* (Florida), January 3, 2009.
Nancy Gibbs	"The Pursuit of Teen Girl Purity," *Time*, July 17, 2008.
Sky Gilbert	"The Promise of Gardasil," *Xtra!*, January 18, 2008.
Globe and Mail (Canada)	"HPV Vaccine," September 20, 2007.
Pius Kamau	"Islam, Condoms and AIDS," *Huffington Post*, August 24, 2008.
Madison Park	"Female Condoms Range from 'Strange' to 'Natural,'" CNN, August 2, 2010. www.cnn.com.
Rob Stein	"Vaccine for Girls Raises Thorny Issues," *Washington Post*, November 7, 2006.
WorldNetDaily	"Death Toll Linked to Gardasil Vaccine Rises," June 30, 2008. www.wnd.com.

OPPOSING
VIEWPOINTS®
SERIES

CHAPTER 4

How Should the Global AIDS Crisis Be Addressed?

Chapter Preface

In 2008, four hundred thousand babies around the world were born with the human immunodeficiency virus (HIV), the virus that causes acquired immune deficiency syndrome (AIDS). Mother-to-child transmission of HIV can occur during pregnancy, labor, delivery, or through breastfeeding—with chances of infection ranging from 20 to 40 percent. However, it can be cut to 1 percent if proper treatment is administered, and access to treatment is rapidly improving worldwide. According to Born HIV Free, a campaign of the Global Fund to Fight AIDS, Tuberculosis and Malaria, the proportion of HIV-positive pregnant women who received antiretroviral treatment rose from 9 percent in 2004 to 45 percent in 2008. "Though there is no cure for HIV and AIDS, it is relatively easy to prevent the transmission of the virus from a mother to her baby, for pregnant women who enter the formal health care system," it states. "This is the first 'end game' in HIV and AIDS: It is possible, feasible, and within our reach." Born HIV Free aims to virtually eliminate all mother-to-child transmissions of HIV by 2015.

Some experts propose that mandatory HIV testing of pregnant women in areas hit hardest by the epidemic should be considered. Bioethicists Udo Schuklenk and Anita Kleinsmidt propose, "If such programs are to be introduced, continuing medical care, including highly active antiretroviral therapy, must be provided and pregnant women must have reasonable alternatives to compulsory testing and treatment," they contend in a 2007 article in the *American Journal of Public Health*. Schuklenk and Kleinsmidt maintain that expanding voluntary testing "is not good public health policy, given resource constraints in countries with high HIV prevalence rates, to divert resources away from testing and treating people toward activities related to health promotion and counseling."

Given the stigma of the disease, such a measure is divisive. "The personal stories of pregnant women and women who have just given birth are too diverse, and the passion and fear associated with HIV are still too intense, to rely on compulsory testing as a successful solution," argues the HIV Law Project, an organization that advocates for those living with HIV and AIDS. "It is precisely in those cases where women fear testing that mandatory or coerced HIV testing drives a wedge between patient and health care provider." In the following chapter, the authors of the viewpoints examine the efforts and policies in battling the global AIDS crisis.

> "[The United States President's Emergency Plan for AIDS Relief] supports the most comprehensive, evidence-based prevention program in the world."

US Global AIDS Policy Is Effective

United States President's Emergency Plan for AIDS Relief (PEPFAR)

The United States President's Emergency Plan for AIDS Relief (PEPFAR) was established by former president George W. Bush in 2003. In the following viewpoint, PEPFAR states that it provides lifesaving services and interventions for nations hardest hit by the AIDS epidemic. As a world health initiative, PEPFAR claims that the size of its funding and scope of its efforts are unrivaled, and it is committed to preventing 7 million infections and caring for 10 million orphans, children, and others affected by AIDS. PEPFAR also asserts that it is a driving force behind several major HIV and AIDS organizations and programs, including the Global Fund to Fight AIDS, Tuberculosis and Malaria and activities of the Joint United Nations Programme on HIV/AIDS.

United States President's Emergency Plan for AIDS Relief (PEPFAR), "Celebrating Life: Fifth Annual Report to Congress on PEPFAR—Highlights Brochure," 2008. Reproduced by permission.

As you read, consider the following questions:

1. How much funding does PEPFAR claim to have committed to the global AIDS epidemic?

2. How can the sexual transmission of HIV be reduced, according to PEPFAR?

3. What are the three dimensions of care for AIDS-stricken populations, in PEPFAR's view?

For more than 25 years, the global community has witnessed the devastating impact of HIV/AIDS [human immunodeficiency virus/acquired immune deficiency syndrome]. Until recently, many wondered whether prevention, treatment and care could ever make a measurable impact, particularly in resource-limited settings where HIV was a death sentence.

Just 5 years ago [in 2003], only 50,000 people living with HIV in all of sub-Saharan Africa were receiving antiretroviral treatment. Recognizing that HIV/AIDS was and is a global health emergency requiring emergency action, the U.S. government, including a bipartisan, bicameral Congress reflected the compassion and generosity of the American people.

Their creation, the U.S. President's Emergency Plan for AIDS Relief (PEPFAR), holds a unique place in the history of public health for its size and scope:

In size, with an original commitment of $15 billion over 5 years, and a final funding level of $18.8 billion, it is the largest international health initiative in history dedicated to a single disease and also the largest development initiative in the world. The first phase of PEPFAR went beyond a commitment to allocating resources to a commitment to achieving results, with ambitious goals to support prevention of 7 million new infections, treatment of 2 million and care for 10 million, including orphans and vulnerable children.

In scope, it is the first large-scale effort to tackle a chronic disease in the developing world. It moves beyond isolated efforts and pendulum swings that led programs to focus on prevention or treatment or care for HIV/AIDS, to sound public health principles—integrated prevention, treatment and care.

The success of PEPFAR is firmly rooted in a commitment to results. Through partnerships between the American people and the people of the countries in which we are privileged to serve—governments, nongovernmental organizations including faith-based organizations and community-based organizations, and the private sector—we are building sustainable systems and empowering individuals, communities, and nations to battle HIV/AIDS.

Together, we have acted quickly. We have already *obligated 92 percent of the funds* initially appropriated to PEPFAR and have *expended or outlayed 68 percent of those resources.*

But success is not best measured in dollars spent. PEPFAR's success is measured in services provided and lives saved.

Partnerships for Prevention

The world cannot defeat this pandemic through treatment and care alone. The UNAIDS [Joint United Nations Programme on HIV/AIDS] *2008 Report on the Global AIDS Epidemic* estimates that there were approximately 2.7 million new HIV infections in 2007.

This indicates that new infections still far outpace the world's ability to add people to treatment. The best approach to the challenges posed by HIV/AIDS is to prevent infection in the first place.

PEPFAR supports the most comprehensive, evidence-based prevention program in the world, targeting interventions based on the epidemiology of HIV infection in each country.

These include reducing sexual transmission with the ABC Strategy (Abstain, Be Faithful, correct and consistent use of

PEPFAR and Gender Realities

We know, for example, that we must place a special emphasis on women and girls to address gender inequities. We must also develop [initiatives] that target men, find men, bring them into care. Strategies that go out into the work setting, where men often are, and engage them in discussions that are peer-led around their role and their relationships with women, and the issues around gender inequities. But not in a talk down, or in a condescending fashion, really more to explore the feelings and the issues that are many hundreds and thousands of years old, and giving perhaps a new frame on which men can begin to think about themselves, begin to question and evolve in their own self-perception and increase the quality in which they engage in their partnerships with women.

As we engage in HIV/AIDS work, we cannot ignore the gender realities—gender inequities, economic dependency, gender-based violence, the lack of educational opportunity and inability to access broader health care in women. PEPFAR [United States President's Emergency Plan for AIDS Relief] is committed to finding ways to focus on these issues and find ways to mainstream these issues into the program areas.

Eric Goosby,
"Remarks Delivered for International AIDS Society Meeting
Special Session on Global HIV Research and Policy Programme
Implementation Under the New United States Administration,
Ambassador Eric Goosby, U.S. Global AIDS Coordinator,"
July 20, 2009. www.pepfar.gov.

Condoms), the prevention of mother-to-child transmission, the transmission of HIV through unsafe blood and medical injections, and male circumcision.

PEPFAR also integrates new prevention methods and technologies as evidence is accumulated and normative guidance provided. It is important for prevention activities to enter the 21st century and keep pace with evidence-based techniques and modalities that have been developed to change human behavior, especially those developed in the private sector for commercial marketing.

Partnerships for Treatment

AIDS is still among the most deadly infectious diseases in the world. In sub-Saharan Africa, the epicenter of the pandemic, it is the leading cause of death. More than 22 million of those infected—more than two-thirds of all people living with HIV/AIDS—live in the region, and approximately 1.7 million people die of AIDS there each year, more than three-quarters of the global total.

However, there is new reason for hope. On a global basis, UNAIDS also estimates that the number of people dying of AIDS-related causes has declined in recent years, from 2.2 million in 2005 to 2.1 million in 2007. This is the first time such a decline has occurred, and the change is due largely to the increased availability of antiretroviral treatment—though improved prevention and care programs have likely contributed as well.

Lives prolonged through treatment benefit not only those on treatment. The ultimate measure of treatment is the daily impact on individual lives, and therefore on their families, communities and nations.

Partnerships for Care

As the pendulum on HIV/AIDS interventions swings between prevention and treatment, it is often care that is lost. Yet care is a critical element of a truly comprehensive approach to fighting HIV/AIDS.

As defined within PEPFAR, there are three key dimensions to care: care for orphans and vulnerable children; care and support (other than antiretroviral treatment) for people infected with or affected by HIV/AIDS; and HIV counseling and testing (which has been counted as Care during the first phase of PEPFAR, but will be counted as part of Prevention for future years). Despite significant progress by PEPFAR in all three areas, much more needs to be done.

Recognizing the central importance of preserving families, PEPFAR focuses on strengthening the capacity of families to protect and care for orphans and vulnerable children by prolonging the lives of parents and caregivers.

PEPFAR also provides "care and support," which refers to the wide range of services other than antiretroviral treatment offered to people living with HIV/AIDS and other affected persons, such as family members. Care and support comprises five categories of services: clinical (including prevention and treatment of opportunistic infections and AIDS-related malignancies, and pain and symptom management), psychological, social, spiritual, and preventive services.

In addition, knowing one's status provides a gateway for critical prevention, treatment, and care. Millions of people must be tested in order for PEPFAR to meet its ambitious prevention, treatment and care goals. PEPFAR programs have worked to ensure that counseling and testing is targeted to those at increased risk of HIV infection such as tuberculosis patients and women seeking services to prevent the transmission of HIV from mother to child.

Working with International Partners

The United States is not the only international partner of host nations. Other key international partners include: the Global Fund [to Fight AIDS, Tuberculosis and Malaria]; the World Bank; United Nations agencies, led by UNAIDS, other national governments; and increasingly the businesses and foundations of the private sector. All of these partners have vital contributions to make to the work of saving lives around the world.

Through PEPFAR, the U.S. government is the first and largest contributor to the Global Fund to Fight AIDS, Tuberculosis and Malaria, a multilateral organization that provides an important vehicle for other nations to increase their commitments on the three diseases. To date, the U.S. government has contributed more than $3.3 billion to the Global Fund. And as of September 2008, PEPFAR and the Global Fund reported supporting antiretroviral treatment for a collective total of 2,952,600 persons.

The United States was a driving force behind the creation of UNAIDS' "Three Ones" principles for support of national HIV/AIDS leadership and continues to support UNAIDS' work in a variety of ways.

Promoting Sustainability and Accountability

PEPFAR supports enduring contributions that build health systems as part of a broader development approach. PEPFAR is working to ensure a sustainable response by building the capacity of public and private institutions in host nations to respond to HIV/AIDS.

With support from PEPFAR, host countries are developing and expanding a culture of accountability that is rooted in country, community, and individual ownership of and participation in the response to HIV/AIDS.

While HIV/AIDS is unmistakably the focus of PEPFAR, the initiative's support for technical and organizational capacity-building for local organizations has important spillover effects that support nations' broader efforts for sustainable development.

> "The underlying problem with [President] Obama's [United States President's Emergency Plan for AIDS Relief] is that ... it is not fully engaging with the constellation of problems associated with HIV and AIDS."

US Global AIDS Policy Is Ineffective

Simon Reid-Henry

Simon Reid-Henry is director of the Centre for the Study of Global Security and Development at Queen Mary, University of London. In the following viewpoint, he states that the successes of the US President's Emergency Plan for AIDS Relief (PEPFAR) may not continue under the Barack Obama administration. Reid-Henry argues that the president's emphasis on sustainable programs instead of emergency interventions covers up harsh cuts in PEPFAR funding. In addition, the author maintains that the underlying problem is that Obama's PEPFAR does not completely address the social ills related to the AIDS epidemic that can be attributed to inequality and poverty.

Simon Reid-Henry, "Obama Stops Thinking Positive," *New Statesman*, January 29, 2010. Reproduced by permission.

As you read, consider the following questions:

1. According to Reid-Henry, what results has PEPFAR achieved?

2. As described in the viewpoint, why is PEPFAR's shift from emergency to sustainable programs a dilemma for funding?

3. What specific problems associated with HIV and AIDS does PEPFAR not fully engage with, as stated by the author?

Once, no one wanted to talk about AIDS [acquired immune deficiency syndrome]. Now the global pandemic commands $14bn [billion] a year, roughly half of all spending on health worldwide. The single most important contributor to AIDS funding is the US President's Emergency Plan for Aids Relief, or PEPFAR for short.

Launched by [former president] George W. Bush in 2003, PEPFAR is the largest financial commitment ever made by any nation to combat a single disease. It wields a budget of $6.7bn for 2010 alone, and claims to have succeeded in putting more than 2.4 million people on antiretroviral therapy, particularly in its "focus" countries (primarily in sub-Saharan Africa). This includes some double-counting with the other major provider of antiretrovirals, the Global Fund to Fight Aids, Tuberculosis and Malaria, but the scope is impressive nonetheless.

The tentative optimism needs to be put in context. There are still 33.4 million people with HIV [human immunodeficiency virus], and, as access to antiretrovirals improves, the number living with the virus continues to climb. Moreover, AIDS-related illnesses remain a major cause of death globally, claiming two million lives a year. Initiatives such as PEPFAR may have provided lifesaving drugs to many, but some global health advocates feel that such organisations are at times more accountable to themselves than to the people enrolled on their programmes. And their sheer scale can disrupt the local health systems of small African countries.

Under Bush, PEPFAR faced more criticism than most. Its initial refusal to purchase and disperse cheaper, generic anti-retrovirals, in preference for only drugs approved by the US Food and Drug Administration, delayed the rollout of lifesaving medicines and demonstrated an unseemly interest in extending the market for overpriced (and usually US-manufactured) drugs. Equally controversial was the Bush-era insistence that a third of the money slated for reducing HIV infection be spent on promoting social values, including abstinence, delay of sexual debut and partner reduction. Such policies are straight out of the Republican book of morals. A focus on monogamy has little value as a preventive tool in countries such as Thailand, where the main mode of transmission is now between married partners.

Self-Selective Choice

With the election of Barack Obama a year ago [in 2008], hopes were high that much of this would change for the better and that PEPFAR might become a more positive standard-bearer in the global fight against HIV and AIDS.

The new president was quick to repeal the most controversial of Bush's global health policies: the "global gag rule"—an outright refusal to fund any organisation that offered (or even provided information about) abortion. And with the appointment of the new US global Aids co-ordinator, Eric Goosby, the emphasis at PEPFAR soon began to fall less on the "emergency" response and more on sustaining existing programmes. Sustainability is important to avoid the emergence of drug resistance, which can render antiretrovirals ineffective.

However, some activists argue that such talk merely disguises the harsh reality of funding cuts. As early as May last year (when his budget plans for 2010 exposed a $1.5bn shortfall in PEPFAR funding), they were arguing that the new presi-

dent had reneged on his campaign promises on AIDS. Since then, Obama has not responded convincingly to their concerns. His new five-year AIDS plan, released at the end of 2009, is silent on the extent to which PEPFAR intends to address concerns about the ongoing lack of transparency in its funding. This worries global health advocates, who wonder if the strategic interests of the US, rather than the health needs of people in its programmes, may be determining PEPFAR's choice of which AIDS programmes to fund and where. Addressing these problems will be difficult, but it is essential that Obama should do so sooner rather than later. For all the importance of treatment, it remains the case that, for every two people being put on antiretrovirals, a further five are being infected.

There are, however, systemic as well as political problems to overcome. PEPFAR allocates a great deal of funding on the basis of evidence it receives from AIDS programmes already in operation. But according to Vinh-Kim Nguyen, a doctor and social scientist with the University of Montreal's department of social and preventive medicine, such evidence of the efficacy of particular interventions can be self-selecting. Organisations promoting treatment interventions (rather than, say, simple prevention or safe sex) find it much easier to get hold of supporting data, because much of the data is taken from individuals already enrolled on programmes being evaluated. Anyone else is excluded, so there is little countervailing evidence (it's hard to provide data on a person not yet infected). But that also makes it difficult to know whether treatment-only approaches to HIV and AIDS are always the most effective.

This should not be taken as an argument for scaling back antiretroviral provision, but it makes it much trickier to gauge how, when and where treatment would be more effective than a less costly alternative.

Social Complications

The underlying problem with Obama's PEPFAR is that—for all the lip service Goosby has paid in recent months—it is not fully engaging with the constellation of problems associated with HIV and AIDS: vulnerability to infection, impoverishment, disempowerment of women, stigmatisation and a persistent AIDS denialism, to name a few. These are social issues that are not always easily quantified, and are often the consequence of relative inequality as much as outright poverty.

In sub-Saharan Africa, women aged between 15 and 24 are more than three times as likely as their male counterparts to be HIV positive; in the United States, the prevalence of HIV among African American males in the District of Columbia ranks alongside that of some of the worst affected countries. The only consistent feature linking sub-epidemics among injecting drug users in the former Soviet republics, men who have sex with men in Asia and heterosexual women in sub-Saharan Africa is the way that HIV can be seen, in each case, to cut along and reinforce preexisting socioeconomic divides.

With funding for many global health initiatives likely to decline in the current economic climate, there is concern that these underlying causes of vulnerability will be pushed further to the margins in a drive for greater statistical accountability and savings in initiatives such as PEPFAR. Pledges to the Global Fund are down. The lives of those who have already been enrolled on antiretroviral programmes in settings where there continues to be a lack of development in local health systems will be put at risk. So too, will the lives of many more people as yet uninfected.

> "The elimination of the need for informed consent and for written proof of consent has multiple legal and ethical implications."

Opt-Out HIV Testing Presents Legal and Ethical Issues

Catherine Hanssens

Catherine Hanssens is executive director and founder of the Center for HIV Law and Policy. In the following viewpoint, Hanssens insists that eschewing written and informed consent for HIV tests presents a host of legal and ethical issues. By forgoing those steps, the patient may not establish a complete understanding with the physician or fully grasp the implications of a positive result, the author claims. Moreover, she insists that HIV-positive individuals still face various forms of discrimination and stigmatization, even in professional and medical settings. Indeed, Hanssens puts forth that health care providers and physicians may be at risk of medical malpractice of patients who suffer the negative consequences of testing positive.

As you read, consider the following questions:

1. How is HIV unlike other conditions and diseases, in the author's opinion?

2. According to the author, what is a way federal agencies discriminate against HIV-positive individuals?

3. What do health care providers face without proof of patient consent to an HIV test, as stated by the author?

In September 2006, the Centers for Disease Control and Prevention (CDC) issued revised recommendations for HIV [human immunodeficiency virus] testing of adults, adolescents, and pregnant women in health care settings. The guidelines recommend that opt-out HIV screening, with no separate written consent, be a routine part of care in all health care settings. The guidelines also somewhat cryptically suggest that, where state or local laws impose more stringent requirements in the areas of counseling, written consent, confirmatory testing, and how to communicate test results to patients, "jurisdictions should consider strategies to best implement these recommendations within current parameters and consider steps to resolve contacts with these recommendations."

Despite the focus on state laws that explicitly address the minimum requirements of HIV testing and confidentiality, legal requirements and liability issues affecting health care professionals and facilities (hereafter referred to as "providers") can arise from a number of other federal and state legal principles implicated by "opt-out" testing. Guidelines that no longer recommended counseling and informed consent for HIV testing for all patients and eliminate the need for written proof that these processes occurred produce legal pitfalls for providers. . . .

Ethics and Patient Consent in the Context of HIV Screening

The elimination of the need for informed consent and for written proof of consent has multiple legal and ethical implications beyond state HIV testing and confidentiality laws. The ultimate objective of screening for a disease is to reduce the morbidity and mortality rates among the people who are screened. As a matter of public health ethics, the primary beneficiaries of the screening must be the individuals who are screened. As the new CDC guidelines emphasize, "[l]inking patients who have received a diagnosis of HIV infection to prevention and care is essential. HIV screening without such linkage confers little or no benefit to the patient." Ethics dictates that HIV testing programs include sufficient funding and case management to ensure that everyone who tests positive for HIV is offered linkage to care as an integral part of the screening process. Although an individual's knowledge of their HIV serostatus may reduce their tendency to engage in conduct that risks transmission, a testing program that identifies this altruistic by-product of testing as its end point is not medically or ethically acceptable.

In addition to general medical and public health ethical considerations, specific professional codes of ethics come into play. For example, replacing informed consent and counseling before and after the test with a passive opt-out system effectively conflicts with the code of ethics of the American Nurses Association, which states that "[t]he nurse strives to provide patients with opportunities to participate in planning care, assures that patients find the plans acceptable, and supports the implementation of the plan".

Informed consent versus general consent. The concept of informed consent, achieved through the process of physician-patient communication, is a legal and ethical obligation spelled out by statute and case law in all 50 states. Informed consent is a legal concept, not a medical concept, and it is central to values of individual autonomy and dignity. Informed consent and general consent are two distinct legal concepts. General consent covers procedures, conditions, and outcomes for which the risks and benefits are generally well known. Informed consent, however, is characterized by a process of communication between a patient and physician that results in the patient's authorization or agreement to undergo a specific medical intervention. A protocol that allows a patient's silence to be construed as consent cannot be characterized as informed consent. Unlike testing for most other infectious diseases, testing for HIV involves risks and benefits that may not be apparent to the patient. Unlike other sexually transmitted diseases and tuberculosis, HIV infection is a lifelong condition, typically requires decades of management with potentially toxic drugs, causes death, and results in social and economic exclusion unparalleled by other current health conditions.

Contextual information and informed consent. The legal definitions and primary elements of informed consent may be fairly consistent, but whether the provider-patient communications process satisfies these definitions hinges on the medical, social, and personal context in which it occurs. Relevant context includes such factors as the invasiveness of a proposed procedure, as well as the extent to which the average reasonable patient is likely to need or want additional information in order to fully understand what is at stake. The individual's age and ability to communicate effectively with the provider are also relevant considerations, as is the routine or emergent nature of the medical intervention (in an emergency, a physician can, without a patient's consent, initiate a medical intervention necessary to preserve life).

Capacity is defined as the ability, irrespective of age, to understand the nature and consequences of a proposed health service. This requires the provider to ensure that the patient currently has the ability to understand the nature and consequences of an intervention, such as an HIV test, and a diagnosis. Capacity and the ability to give legally adequate consent can be compromised as a consequence of substance abuse, mental impairment, language limitations, or even the medical condition serving as the primary reason for presenting for care.

It is a common misunderstanding that the very minor physical risks of an HIV test are the only factors relevant to informed consent. On the contrary, adverse effects on emotional health and mental health are risks that should be addressed as part of securing legally adequate consent. Accordingly, informed consent to HIV testing would include an understanding of the risks of negative "labeling" and of the adverse psychological effects of a positive test result or an AIDS [acquired immune deficiency syndrome] diagnosis.

Courts' approaches to informed consent. Courts take two distinct approaches to the issue of informed consent. In 1972, a federal appeals court first articulated the modern "reasonable patient" standard under which the necessary information on risks is determined by what a reasonable person in that patient's position would want to know. Approximately half of US states have adopted this approach. Under the older, traditional approach, the duty to disclose information relevant to a procedure is determined by what a "reasonable physician" would disclose under similar circumstances.

The modern approach reflects the view that the standard of disclosure exercised by many in the medical profession bears little relationship to the information a patient actually needs to make an informed choice. Because the patient bears the consequences of a medical diagnosis or treatment, it is the patient's right to know all the material facts. Supporters of the reasonable patient standard argue that physicians' inclination to offer more-cursory disclosures renders them unsuited to determine the parameters of a patient's right to know. The right to know is, after all, a nonmedical issue and, as such, is outside the physician's professional expertise. A standard that determines a doctor's duty to inform a patient on the basis of that patient's need or desire to know serves to encourage less authoritarian and, ultimately, more-productive relationships between physicians and their patients.

The trend towards a patient-based standard of consent is consistent with consensus reflected in international law. The Convention on Human Rights and Biomedicine states that a patient must be given the correct information about the nature and purpose, consequences, and risks of a medical intervention.

Stigmatization and Discrimination: Continuing Consequences for People with HIV Infection

The ongoing consequences of a positive HIV test result are an important element in assessing the legal and ethical relevance of informed consent. The legitimacy of patient concerns about negative labeling—a potential harmful consequence of screening—is borne out by the stigmatization and discrimination still strongly associated with a positive test result. Violation of the civil rights of people with HIV infection and AIDS remains widespread throughout the United States. Surveys continue to document frequent denials of medical treatment, loss of parental rights, workplace discrimination, exclusion from nursing homes and residential facilities, and violations of privacy. In fact, a December 2006 study documented that 25%–50% of skilled nursing facilities, obstetricians, and cosmetic surgeons in Los Angeles County deny treatment to HIV-positive patients.

A recent lawsuit for discrimination, in which emergency medical technicians in Philadelphia allegedly refused to touch an acutely ill HIV-infected person or help him onto a stretcher, illustrates the problem. Research has demonstrated continued social ostracism of people infected with HIV; some studies showed that concerns about the impact of stigmatization and discrimination on individuals, their families, and their communities affect the decision to get tested. A 2004 study of violence against young homosexual men found they were more likely to experience verbal harassment, discrimination, and physical violence if they were HIV positive.

HIV-associated stigmatization and discrimination are reinforced by government agencies with exclusionary policies that lack sound scientific basis. CDC guidelines still recommend unfounded restrictions on practices of health care workers infected with HIV. Other federal agencies, such as the State Department, the Federal Aviation Administration, the Peace Corps, and all branches of the military, continue to restrict the employment or licensing of healthy qualified people with HIV infection. A number of states prohibit the licensing of HIV-infected persons for professions such as barbering, massage therapy, and home health care. Twenty-four states criminalize the sexual activity of people with HIV, with most states imposing terms of imprisonment regardless of whether there was mutual consent, prophylaxis [such as a condom] was used, or HIV transmission occurred.

Recent studies also document that many people of color who support the notion of routinely offered HIV testing are deterred from being tested, because of concerns about privacy and stigmatization and distrust or misconceptions about the importance of testing. Some persons even avoid testing, because they believe that they could become infected with HIV during the test. A recent national study of 2466 HIV-infected adults receiving care in the United States showed that 25% believed their clinicians discriminated against them after they first tested positive.

New CDC Guidelines: Potential Legal Hurdles and Pitfalls

Reactive, unrefined application of the new CDC guidelines could trigger a range of legal claims. Institutional patterns of HIV testing without linkage to care, as well as evidence of racial disparities in linkages to care for those who test positive, could provide the basis for a disability or race-based discrimination claim. Moreover, amending state law is a protracted process and could result in dilution of important confidentiality protections.

Without proof of patient consent, health care providers could face liability regarding claims of failure to get informed consent for patients whose general capacity to provide consent may be in question, such as adolescents, emergency department patients, immigrants, and people with language barriers.

An abridged pretest counseling and consent process can reinforce a claim of medical malpractice. For individuals who have experienced negative consequences as a result of a positive or false-positive HIV test, an inadequate explanation of the test—its purpose, benefits, limitations, and emotional and legal consequences and the meaning and medical significance of a posture and negative test result—can result in successful malpractice claims. Inadequate physician communication is one of the most common factors in patients' decisions to file claims against their doctors.

The risk of legal liability or ethical conflicts following the negative consequences of a positive HIV test is heightened in vulnerable patients for whom a positive HIV test poses an increased social risk. Typical fallout of a positive test result can include domestic violence, loss of housing, loss of employment or job opportunities, and psychological trauma.

Limited knowledge of state and HIV confidentiality laws is another potential source of liability for physicians. Inappropriate disclosures by staff of state facilities may also trigger constitutional-privacy claims. In correctional settings, inmates may have claims relating to inadequate medical care or privacy violations, if HIV testing is conducted without privacy or with coercion, without protections against disclosure to staff and inmates, or without access to medications and related care during incarceration and prior to release.

> *"Until we have universal testing and mandatory reporting, tracing and treatment, the government is failing to fulfill its obligation to protect the public health interests of America's uninfected, regardless of race or ethnicity."*

Mandatory HIV Testing Will Save Lives

Sanford F. Kuvin

In the following viewpoint, Sanford F. Kuvin advocates mandatory testing of HIV for all risk groups. According to him, from 20 to 40 percent of HIV-positive Americans are unaware of their status, significantly driving the epidemic among blacks. Additionally, Kuvin maintains that voluntary testing—as shown through current infection rates—is ineffective. The federal government shields Americans from flu epidemics and tuberculosis through universal screening, he contends, and they have a right to the same protection against HIV. The author is founder and international chair of the Kuvin Center for the Study of Infectious and Tropical Diseases at the Hebrew University of Jerusalem.

Sanford F. Kuvin, "Our Country Is Failing the AIDS Test," *Washington Post*, December 1, 2008. Reproduced by permission.

As you read, consider the following questions:

1. How can mandatory HIV testing and treatment benefit Africa, as stated by Kuvin?

2. What is not required if a patient tests positive for HIV, as described by the author?

3. How should mandatory HIV screening be carried out, as recommended by Kuvin?

A IDS [acquired immune deficiency syndrome] remains the world's No. 1 health threat and in the United States is a grave risk to black people in particular. As Phill Wilson, executive director of the Black AIDS Institute, put it, "AIDS in America is a black disease ... about half of the just over 1 million Americans living with HIV [human immunodeficiency virus] or AIDS are black."

Yet the disaster of AIDS in black or white America does not have to be this way. While a cure is still years away, a nation with U.S. literacy rates and levels of cultural and public health sophistication is capable of greatly reducing its number of new infections. So why are new AIDS cases, particularly among blacks in urban areas, outpacing gains in control, treatment or education among high-risk groups?

The answer lies in the unwillingness of the Centers for Disease Control and Prevention [CDC] to adopt control measures, including routine mandatory testing among broad age groups. Any time blood samples are taken from U.S. residents ages 13 to 64, such as in an emergency room, physicians should have the right to scan for HIV. For those who don't regularly visit a doctor, blood tests could be scheduled, with the results recorded by states and the CDC. As the *Post* reported last week [in November 2008], a recent study in the *Lancet* concluded that such measures, accompanied by treatment for all those who are HIV positive, have the potential to

Preserving Lives over Counseling

One could argue that, as opposed to advocating mandatory testing and treatment, we should aim to increase the number of women who voluntarily undergo testing and treatment. We should expand educational programs and persuade rather than force pregnant women to be tested and treated. We believe that although such programs are valuable, it is not good public health policy, given resource constraints in countries with high HIV prevalence rates, to divert resources away from testing and treating people toward activities related to health promotion and counseling. In cases of conflicting needs and limited resources, preserving lives must take priority over counseling.

Udo Schuklenk and Anita Kleinsmidt,
"Rethinking Mandatory HIV Testing During Pregnancy in Areas
with High HIV Prevalence Rates: Ethical and Policy Issues,"
American Journal of Public Health, *July 2007.*

end the AIDS epidemic in Africa within a decade. The effects are likely to be faster in this country.

Not Even Aware

When bird flu was a threat a few years ago, strict mandatory testing measures were implemented in high-risk areas, greatly reducing the threat of an epidemic. But unlike bird flu, which presents symptoms quickly, HIV can remain undetected for years. Because we do not test all risk groups, 20 to 40 percent of Americans who are HIV positive are not even aware that they are infected, and they often pass on the virus. This alone significantly contributes to the epidemic among black Americans.

HIV is spread only by blood, sex, and needles and during pregnancy, but within those parameters, people are equally susceptible, regardless of gender, age, color or social status. So when the CDC, in a public policy about-face, recommended in 2006 that doctors offer HIV tests not just to high-risk patients but as part of routine medical care to everyone ages 13 to 64, it was a giant step forward. But nothing requires physicians to comply with this recommendation. And U.S. infection rates show that voluntary testing has failed to stem the tide of this disease.

Today not even pregnant women in America are regularly tested for HIV. They must ask to be and it's understandable that few people are interested in receiving such potentially frightening information. Sadly, when a test is positive, there is no mandatory treatment or counseling for the patient, nor does federal law require that a patient's sexual partners be notified or tested.

All U.S. measures regarding HIV testing, treatment and tracing are voluntary—a policy that has resulted in an increase in AIDS cases, many of which could have been prevented by simple public health initiatives. Blood testing should be mandatory once or twice a year when people visit a doctor's office or hospital. Testing already is mandatory in blood banks and the military, and it is a policy of many insurance companies. Other routine blood tests are done without patients' explicit permission when doctors deem it advisable; it should be the same with HIV.

The Same Public Health Protection

It might surprise many to learn that the paradigm of excellent AIDS control can be found in Cuba, which discovered this sexually transmitted disease—long before it was named— among its soldiers when they returned from Angola in the 1960s. Mandatory testing, tracing and treatment brought that nation the lowest AIDS rate in the Western world.

To be clear: No Americans need to be quarantined for HIV/AIDS. But all citizens are entitled to the same public health protection under the law that is already afforded them against tuberculosis or bird flu.

Until we have universal testing and mandatory reporting, tracing and treatment, the government is failing to fulfill its obligation to protect the public health interests of America's uninfected, regardless of race or ethnicity. The United States has the opportunity to prolong uncountable numbers of lives and protect millions of others. America should choose to lead—and leave behind its ineffective public health policy.

> "Should this prove to be a forerunner to a usable vaccine, it would be the second big game-changer in AIDS research."

The Experimental HIV Vaccine Is Promising

Gautam Naik

Gautam Naik is a staff reporter at the Wall Street Journal. *In the following viewpoint, Naik states that a medical trial in Thailand saw a breakthrough in the development of an HIV vaccine. The combination of two vaccines, the author writes, cut the chance of infection among more than sixteen thousand volunteers by 31 percent, renewing the debate of whether funding should go into HIV prevention or long-term treatment. For researchers, the challenges that remain are to figure out why this vaccine regimen was effective while others failed, why it worked for some volunteers and not others, how long the vaccine protects, and if the benchmark achieved in the trial can be improved, Naik writes.*

Gautam Naik, "Vaccine Shows Promise in Preventing HIV Infection," *Wall Street Journal*, September 25, 2009. Reproduced by permission.

As you read, consider the following questions:

1. As stated by Naik, what are the figures from the Thailand trial?

2. What is the background of combining HIV vaccines in trials, as described by Naik?

3. Why may the vaccine not be applicable or effective in Africa, according to Naik?

The first vaccine to show any sign of preventing the spread of HIV has provided the most encouragement since the 1990s in the three-decades quest to stem the global AIDS [acquired immune deficiency syndrome] epidemic.

Results of a trial involving more than 16,000 adults in Thailand indicate the vaccine regimen was safe and reduced by 31% the chance of infection with the AIDS-causing human immunodeficiency virus, or HIV, according to the U.S. National Institutes of Health [NIH], which helped fund the study.

Though that 31% is modest, it has heartened public health experts and scientists. It is the first time a vaccine has been shown to confer any HIV protection at all. Should this prove to be a forerunner to a usable vaccine, it would be the second big game-changer in AIDS research since the mid-1990s, when potent new "drug cocktails"—a mix of protease inhibitors and other antiretrovirals—turned AIDS from a virtual death sentence into a chronic but manageable disease for many patients.

"Antiretrovirals are obviously a very important tool against AIDS, but preventing infections is the highest priority," said Saladin Osmanov, coordinator of the HIV-vaccine initiative overseen by the World Health Organization and UNAIDS [Joint United Nations Programme on HIV/AIDS], an arm of the United Nations [UN]. "The results from Thailand are modest, but they're a very good start" toward a vaccine.

The Best Long-Term Hope

Emerging during the last quarter of the twentieth century, the HIV [human immunodeficiency virus] pandemic has now extended into the twenty-first century and is still progressing. As has been the case with many other infectious diseases, a safe, effective and accessible preventive vaccine represents the best long-term hope for control of the HIV pandemic. The development of an HIV vaccine, however, has faced a number of difficult scientific challenges that have been compounded by additional logistical and financial difficulties. To address the scientific challenges, there is a need to coordinate the current research effort better so that the scientific creativity of individual investigators is complemented by a more global, collaborative strategy aimed at developing and testing novel candidate vaccines faster and more efficiently.

Eduard J. Beck, Nicholas Mays,
Alan W. Whiteside, José M. Zuniga, eds.,
The HIV Pandemic: Local and Global Implications,
New York: Oxford University Press, 2006.

The Beginning of the Effort

The surprisingly good data from Thailand could reignite an old debate about how to respond to AIDS globally: Put more money and resources into prevention with vaccines, or focus more on drugs that prolong the lives of those already infected.

About 33 million people were living with HIV worldwide in 2007, the most recent year for which statistics were available, according to the UN. That same year, about two million people died of AIDS and 2.7 million more became infected.

For now, the scientists will try to figure out why the latest vaccine worked when previous ones failed, and why it worked for some participants and not others. They also need to understand how long the vaccine's protection lasts and whether its efficacy can be boosted beyond 31%.

"This is the beginning of the effort," said Anthony Fauci, director of the National Institute of Allergy and Infectious Diseases [NIAID], which is part of the NIH. "It has opened up a door for us to ask some very important fundamental science questions as well as some clinical questions."

In the three-year experiment, 74 of 8,198 people who received placebo shots became infected with HIV compared with 51 of 8,197 people who received the vaccine, suggesting the vaccine regimen could have reduced the risk of being infected by 31%.

The NIH said the results are statistically significant. However, researchers involved in the trial haven't yet publicly released any detailed data. Vital details are expected to be presented at an AIDS-vaccine conference in Paris next month [October 2009].

Two Vaccines

The regimen consists of two vaccines. One is a primer dose made by Sanofi Pasteur, a division of Sanofi-Aventis SA of France. The other is a booster dose developed by VaxGen Inc. and now licensed to Global Solutions for Infectious Diseases [GSID], of South San Francisco, Calif.

"It's unclear why two vaccines that have been separately tested and had little activity or none, when put together seem to give 30% protection," said Barry Bloom, former dean of the Harvard School of Public Health. "That's a puzzlement."

The idea of combining two vaccines to bolster the breadth and potency of an immune response is an old one. Such combinations had worked in animal models in the 1990s, when Sanofi combined its HIV vaccine with a booster. The decision to try this in the Thai trial was made by the key partners, including Sanofi Pasteur, the U.S. Army, the NIH and VaxGen, according to Jim Tartaglia, vice president of R&D at Sanofi Pasteur.

The vaccine was specially designed for use in Thailand because it is based on the subtype B and E strains of HIV common there. Thus, it isn't clear whether it would work in Africa, where subtypes A, C and D predominate. Two-thirds of the 33 million people with HIV live in Africa, and 75% of all AIDS deaths in 2007 occurred there. One way around the problem is to test an Africa-specific vaccine incorporating local HIV subtypes.

The U.S. Army's involvement in a vaccine trial isn't unusual. On its website, the U.S. Military HIV Research Program notes that its researchers have often been involved in finding fixes for infectious diseases that affect American forces. "HIV continues to pose a significant and persistent threat in terms of readiness and force protection, and may affect the stability and security of many nation-states," it reads.

Low Expectations

There were low expectations for the Thai trial, largely due to the dismal track record. There have been more than 100 vaccine trials since 1987; one of the biggest setbacks occurred in 2007, when Merck & Co. ended a closely watched trial.

The Thai trial was set up to see not only whether the vaccine could prevent infections but also whether it could lower the viral load which, in turn, has an effect on how the disease progresses. However, vaccinated patients who still became infected didn't have lower levels of the HIV virus than patients who received the placebo and became infected.

Cate Hankins, chief scientific adviser at UNAIDS, noted that only 125 people who participated in the trial ended up with HIV and said a larger sample might have revealed different results about viral loads.

The trial enrolled men and women 18 to 30 years old drawn from the general population, at various levels of HIV risk. Those who contracted the virus have been provided with medical care and treatment. The trial was sponsored by the U.S. Army and conducted by the Thailand Ministry of Public Health, collaborating with NIAID, Sanofi Pasteur, GSID and others.

> *"A healthy immune system can fight off HIV in the same way it fights off a cold virus."*

An HIV Vaccine Is Unnecessary

Mike Adams

In the following viewpoint, Mike Adams alleges that an HIV vaccine is unnecessary and even harmful. Adams upholds that the immune system is capable of defending the body against HIV, and it can be exposed to the virus without becoming infected. Consequently, an HIV immunization is not medically necessary, and experimental vaccines produce false HIV positives in up to 86 percent of subjects, he adds. Furthermore, a false-positive status not only stigmatizes but also deceives people into seeking expensive, dangerous antiviral drugs and treatment, which drives the profits of pharmaceutical companies, the author says. Adams is editor and writer for NaturalNews.com, an independent website for health and natural living.

As you read, consider the following questions:

1. Why are HIV tests unreliable, as claimed by Adams?

Mike Adams, "HIV Vaccines Cause 50 Percent False Positive Rate in HIV Tests," Natural-News, July 20, 2010. Reproduced by permission.

2. According to the author, what are three repercussions a positive HIV result from a vaccine can have on people's lives?

3. How is AIDS prevention like mammograms, in the author's opinion?

It may come as a big surprise to most people, but HIV [human immunodeficiency virus] tests given to people today don't actually test for the presence of the HIV virus. Rather, they test for the presence of HIV *antibodies* that the immune system creates to *defend* itself against HIV. And just because you have HIV antibodies doesn't mean you actually carry HIV. In some circumstances, up to 50 percent of HIV positives are false, causing havoc with the lives of those patients who are falsely accused of being "HIV positive."

This startling fact was revealed in a recent study that's being published in the July 21 [2010] issue of the *Journal of the American Medical Association*. It shows that patients who are recruited for HIV vaccine trials often end up testing positive for HIV even though they were only exposed to the vaccine, not the virus.

"Almost half of HIV-negative people who participate in clinical trials for HIV vaccines end up testing positive on routine HIV tests—even though they're not actually infected" reports *U.S. News & World Report*.

Some vaccines caused a false-positive rate of over 86 percent.

HIV Tests Lack Credibility

What this new study clearly demonstrates is the complete lack of scientific credibility of common HIV tests. It also demonstrates the dangers of getting vaccinated against HIV, because the mere act of receiving an HIV vaccination may cause you to test positive for HIV, which, in turn, can have many serious repercussions in your life:

- You may be denied employment because tests show you are "HIV positive."

- You may be denied health insurance coverage or be charged significantly more than others for the same coverage.

- You may be denied residence in other countries, as many countries require HIV tests for prospective new residency.

- You may be falsely accused of having AIDS [acquired immune deficiency syndrome] by health authorities who archive your medical records and use them against you.

- You may be arrested and sent to prison, accused of attempted murder, by sleeping with someone and not telling them you were HIV positive (even though you don't have AIDS).

- You may be denied the opportunity to participate in certain professions or activities (such as sporting events).

- You may be socially stigmatized and thought of as an "AIDS carrier."

- You may be shunned by sex partners or a spouse.

All this could happen to you if you receive an HIV vaccine—*even if you don't carry the HIV virus!*

HIV and AIDS Vaccines Are Medically Unnecessary

We have already established here on NaturalNews that HIV/ AIDS vaccines are medically unnecessary. A healthy immune system can fight off HIV in the same way it fights off a cold virus. But don't just take my word for it; listen to the words of

Dr. Luc Montagnier, the Nobel Prize–winning virologist credited with the co-discovery of HIV. He says:

"We can be exposed to HIV many times without being ... infected. Our immune system creates [antibodies] within a few weeks, if you have a good immune system."

Your own body, in other words, can protect itself from HIV exposure with the same technology your body uses to save your life from influenza every year: Your immune system.

HIV vaccines, then, are entirely unnecessary. Vaccines are Big Pharma's [the pharmaceutical industry's] way of selling you something you don't need by trying to convince you that you might die without it. And when it comes to AIDS, Big Pharma has done a terrific job of scaring people into pursuing all kinds of unnecessary treatments that only harm their health in the long run.

In this way, the AIDS industry is much like the breast cancer industry ... or the prostate cancer industry: Most of what they push onto people is medically unjustified, scientifically unproven and actually harms more people than it helps. But it's great for generating more profits for Big Pharma.

And that's the point of all this. AIDS is just another profit center for the drug industry, and if their vaccines actually cause you to test positive for HIV, that's even better for their profits because some percentage of those people who test positive are probably going to be put on antiretroviral drugs to treat HIV, and those drugs are massive profit centers for Big Pharma.

Western Medicine Causes Disease Instead of Curing It

See, what's really fascinating here is that the AIDS industry demonstrates yet again how the medical industry *causes* the very diseases it claims to be treating. Mammograms—which claim to "detect" breast cancer—actually *cause* breast cancer.

So if you get enough mammograms, eventually you'll develop breast cancer and require expensive cancer treatments.

The AIDS industry now works in much the same way: If you get an HIV vaccine, chances are you're then going to test positive for being an HIV carrier, and you'll become an "AIDS patient" who spends your life savings on needless drugs and other expensive treatments for a disease you don't even have!

The psychiatric industry works the same way, too: It actually *invents* fictitious diseases such as "oppositional defiance disorder" (which means disagreeing with authority) and then tries to put children and adults on mind-altering psychotropic drugs to "treat" that disease.

The more you look into the industries of pharmaceuticals and vaccines, the more you realize the whole business is just *full of bunk*. Their vaccines don't work, their tests produce false positives and their pharmaceuticals can kill you.

That's why it's so much easier to just take care of your own health, build up a healthy immune system, avoid exposure to toxic chemicals and let your body's miraculous immune system do the job for you.

Periodical and Internet Sources Bibliography

The following articles have been selected to supplement the diverse views presented in this chapter.

Russell Armstrong	"Mandatory HIV Testing in Pregnancy: Is There Ever a Time?" *Developing World Bioethics*, September 19, 2007.
Simeon Bennett and Tom Randall	"AIDS Drugs Flow to the Third World," *BusinessWeek*, August 5, 2010.
Heather D. Boonstra	"Renewing a Focus on Prevention in U.S. Global AIDS Policy," *Guttmacher Policy Review*, Fall 2007.
Kim Carollo	"HIV Antibody Finding May Be New Piece to AIDS Puzzle," ABC News, July 8, 2010. http://abcnews.go.com.
Gary Daffin and Laura Kogelman	"'Opt-Out' HIV Testing: A Better Paradigm in the Real World," *Boston Banner*, November 26, 2009.
Karen Kaplan and Thomas H. Maugh II	"HIV Vaccine Feat Leaves More Questions than Answers," *Los Angeles Times*, September 25, 2009.
Donald G. McNeil Jr.	"Obama Is Criticized on AIDS Program," *New York Times*, December 8, 2009.
Alice Park	"David Ho: The Man Who Could Beat AIDS," *Time*, January 25, 2010.
Katie Paul	"The PEPFAR Paradox," *Newsweek*, November 30, 2009.
Voice of America	"Health Economist Says New US Administration Must Modify HIV AIDS Policy," November 4, 2008. www.voanews.com.

For Further Discussion

Chapter 1

1. Grant Stoddard states that up to 75 percent of sexually active Americans are infected with the human papillomavirus (HPV). In your opinion, does this undermine his position that a growing number of adults have irrational fears about sexually transmitted diseases (STDs)? Why or why not?

2. Carol Midgley contends that young gay men have become complacent about HIV and AIDS. In your view, does Tony Valenzuela's viewpoint reflect such attitudes toward the disease? Cite examples from the texts to explain your answer.

3. Craig Timberg reports that the United Nations overestimated the world population infected with HIV as well as the scope of the epidemic. In your opinion, does this scale back the urgency of HIV in Africa? Use examples from the viewpoints to support your response.

Chapter 2

1. Cory Richards contends that considerable evidence has shown that programs including information on contraception and abstinence reduce the number of sexual partners among teenagers and "delay the onset of sexual activity." Do you agree with his assessment? Why or why not?

2. In your view, does Miriam Grossman persuasively argue that adolescents are incapable of using condoms and other forms of protection? Why or why not?

Chapter 3

1. In your view, do Robert Rector and Kirk Johnson successfully counter the claims that virginity pledges do not cut rates of STD infections? Cite examples from the viewpoints to explain your answer.

2. Heather Corinna asserts that condoms do not offer 100 percent protection from some STDs but argues against abstinence if it impairs a person's quality of life. In your opinion, does Corinna send a mixed message about safe sex? Why or why not?

Chapter 4

1. Simon Reid-Henry proposes that the successes of the US President's Emergency Plan for AIDS Relief (PEPFAR) under former president George W. Bush are relative compared to the current state of the HIV/AIDS epidemic. Do you agree or disagree with the author? Use examples from the texts to support your response.

2. Do you agree or disagree with Sanford F. Kuvin that the government is responsible for protecting individuals from HIV? Why or why not?

3. Mike Adams states that the immune system can fend off exposure to HIV. In your opinion, does Adams back his claim with reliable scientific evidence? Cite examples from the viewpoint to explain your answer.

Organizations to Contact

The editors have compiled the following list of organizations concerned with the issues debated in this book. The descriptions are derived from materials provided by the organizations. All have publications or information available for interested readers. The list was compiled on the date of publication of the present volume; the information provided here may change. Be aware that many organizations take several weeks or longer to respond to inquiries, so allow as much time as possible.

Alive and Well AIDS Alternatives
11684 Ventura Boulevard, Studio City, CA   91604
(818) 780-1875 • fax: (818) 780-7093
e-mail: info@aliveandwell.org
website: www.aliveandwell.org

Alive and Well AIDS Alternatives is an organization that presents information that questions the validity of many of the common assumptions about HIV and AIDS, including the accuracy of HIV tests and the effectiveness of AIDS drug treatments. The organization's website features information on whether a link exists between HIV and AIDS, and the site also addresses facts and myths about AIDS drugs.

American Social Health Association (ASHA)
PO Box 13827, Research Triangle Park, NC   27709
(919) 361-8400 • fax: (919) 361-8425
e-mail: info@ashastd.org
website: www.ashastd.org

The American Social Health Association (ASHA) is a nonprofit organization that works to improve public health outcomes and is a leading authority on information pertaining to sexually transmitted diseases (STDs). Facts and statistics about STDs are available on ASHA's website. The organization's publications include *What You Should Know About Chlamydia*; *Hepatitis: Knowing the Differences Between A, B, and C*; and *Syphilis: A Serious Disease, A Simple Cure.*

amfAR: The Foundation for AIDS Research

120 Wall Street, 13th Floor, New York, NY   10005-3908
(212) 806-1600 • fax: (212) 806-1601
website: www.amfar.org

amfAR: The Foundation for AIDS Research is a nonprofit organization that supports HIV/AIDS research, treatment education, and AIDS prevention. Its mission is to prevent HIV infection and to protect the human rights of everyone who is affected by the epidemic. The organization publishes an electronic newsletter, reports on HIV/AIDS in Asia and the Pacific, an annual report, and several issue briefs.

Canadian AIDS Society (CAS)

190 O'Connor Street, Suite 800, Ottawa, ON   K2P 2R3
  Canada
(613) 230-3580 • fax: (613) 563-4998
e-mail: casinfo@cdnaids.ca
website: www.cdnaids.ca

The Canadian AIDS Society (CAS) is a national coalition of more than 120 community-based AIDS organizations across Canada. The society is dedicated to improving the lives of people living with HIV/AIDS and strengthening Canada's response to the epidemic. CAS publishes position papers, including *Anti-Retroviral Therapy (ART) as Prevention*, fact sheets, and reports.

Centers for Disease Control and Prevention (CDC)— Sexually Transmitted Diseases

1600 Clifton Road, Atlanta, GA   30333
(800) 232-4636
e-mail: cdcinfo@cdc.gov
website: www.cdc.gov/std

The Centers for Disease Control and Prevention (CDC) is one of the major components of the Department of Health and Human Services. Its purpose is to lead public health efforts to prevent and control the spread of infectious and chronic diseases. Its section on sexually transmitted diseases (STDs) provides information on various infectious diseases and includes fact sheets and statistics as well as links to publications.

Concerned Women for America (CWA)

1015 Fifteenth Street NW, Suite 1100, Washington, DC   20005
(202) 488-7000 • fax: (202) 488-0806
website: www.cwfa.org

Concerned Women for America (CWA) aims to promote biblical values throughout society to reverse what it considers the decline in America's moral values. CWA supports abstinence-only sexual education and questions the efficacy of condoms in preventing sexually transmitted diseases (STDs). The organization publishes the magazine *Family Voice* and brochures including "What Your Teacher Didn't Tell You About Abstinence."

Family Health International (FHI)

2224 East North Carolina Highway 54, Durham, NC   27713
(919) 544-7040 • fax: (919) 544-7261
website: www.fhi.org

The mission of Family Health International (FHI) is to improve public health throughout the world through research and education. The organization works with research institutions, government organizations, and the private sector to achieve this goal. The FHI also aims to prevent the spread of sexually transmitted diseases (STDs) and provide care for people affected by those diseases. Books and reports are available on the website, including "Empowered by Faith" and *The Handbook on Pædiatric AIDS in Africa*.

Family Research Council (FRC)

801 G Street NW, Washington, DC   20001

(202) 393-2100 • fax: (202) 393-2134
website: www.frc.org

The Family Research Council (FRC) develops public policy that upholds the institutions of marriage and family; among the issues it supports is abstinence-only education. Publications on AIDS and abstinence-only education, including "Abstinence Education Is the Key" and "Abstinence Works: Let's Give It a Chance," are available on the FRC's website.

Gay Men's Health Crisis (GMHC)

119 West Twenty-fourth Street, New York, NY   10011
(212) 367-1000
website: www.gmhc.org

Gay Men's Health Crisis (GMHC) is an organization that helps lead the fight against AIDS. It aims to reduce the spread of HIV; improve the health and independence of people with HIV; and ensure that the prevention, treatment, and cure of HIV remain a national priority. The organization publishes fact sheets and the quarterly magazine *Treatment Issues*. The website provides information on treatment, testing, and other sexually transmitted diseases (STDs).

Guttmacher Institute

125 Maiden Lane, 7th Floor, New York, NY   10038
(800) 355-0244 • fax: (212) 248-1951
e-mail: info@guttmacher.org
website: www.guttmacher.org

The mission of the Guttmacher Institute is to use public education, policy analysis, and social science research to promote sound policy and create new ideas about sexual health. It aims to improve access to information about sexually transmitted diseases (STDs). The organization publishes the periodicals *Perspectives on Sexual and Reproductive Health, International Perspectives on Sexual and Reproductive Health,* and *Guttmacher Policy Review*. The website features a section on STDs that includes fact sheets, policy briefs, articles, and reports.

International AIDS Society (IAS)
Avenue Louis Casaï 71, PO Box 28, Cointrin
Geneva   CH-1216
  Switzerland
+41-(0)22-7 100 800 • fax: +41-(0)22-7 100 899
website: www.iasociety.org

The International AIDS Society (IAS) is a worldwide independent association of HIV/AIDS professionals who are working to prevent, treat, and control the epidemic. The society organizes the International AIDS Conference. IAS publishes a newsletter and annual reports, and its website links to articles about AIDS.

Planned Parenthood Federation of America
434 West Thirty-third Street, New York, NY   10001
(212) 541-7800 • fax: (212) 245-1845
website: www.plannedparenthood.org

For more than ninety years, Planned Parenthood Federation of America has promoted women's health and well-being based on the individual's right to make informed, independent decisions about health, sex, and family planning. Its website provides information on sexually transmitted diseases (STDs), birth control, and the sexual health of both men and women.

Sexuality Information and Education Council of the United States (SIECUS)
90 John Street, Suite 402, New York, NY   10038
(212) 819-9770 • fax: (212) 819-9776
website: www.siecus.org

The Sexuality Information and Education Council of the United States (SIECUS) is an organization that provides information for parents, health professionals, educators, and communities to ensure that all individuals receive comprehensive information about sexuality. SIECUS also works to have sound public policy developed on sexuality-related issues. The council publishes special reports and newsletters.

World Health Organization (WHO)

Avenue Appia 20, Geneva 27   1211
  Switzerland
+41 22 791 21 11 • fax: + 41 22 791 31 11
e-mail: info@who.int
website: www.who.int

The World Health Organization (WHO) is the United Nations' specialized agency for health. The objective of WHO is to help all people achieve the highest possible level of health. The website has links to fact sheets and publications about HIV and AIDS, including "Addressing Violence Against Women and HIV/AIDS: What Works?" and "HIV/AIDS—Stand Up for Human Rights."

Bibliography of Books

Henry H. Bauer   *The Origin, Persistence and Failings of HIV/AIDS Theory.* Jefferson, NC: McFarland & Co., 2007.

Marvelyn Brown and Courtney E. Martin   *The Naked Truth: Young, Beautiful, and (HIV) Positive.* New York: Amistad, 2008.

Aine Collier   *The Humble Little Condom: A History.* New York: Prometheus Books, 2007.

Bonnie L. Diraimondo   *Any Mother's Daughter: One Woman's Lifelong Struggle with HPV (Human Papillomavirus).* Bloomington, IN: AuthorHouse, 2010.

Don S. Dizon and Michael L. Krychman   *Questions & Answers About Human Papilloma Virus.* Sudbury, MA: Jones and Bartlett Publishers, 2011.

Charles Ebel and Anna Wald   *Managing Herpes: Living and Loving with HSV.* Research Triangle Park, NC: American Social Health Association, 2007.

Jonathan Engel   *The Epidemic: A Global History of AIDS.* New York: Smithsonian Books/Collins, 2006.

Helen Epstein   *The Invisible Cure: Why We Are Losing the Fight Against AIDS in Africa.* New York: Picador, 2008.

Douglas A. Feldman — *Ethnicity and Health Care Delivery: Sexually Transmitted Diseases.* Saarbrücken, Germany: Lambert Academic Publishing, 2009.

Samuel Frimpong — *STD/HIV Prevention Action: Let's Protect Each Other.* Bloomington, IN: iUniverse, 2010.

Jill Grimes — *Seductive Delusions: How Everyday People Catch STDs.* Baltimore, MD: Johns Hopkins University Press, 2008.

Miriam Grossman — *Unprotected: A Campus Psychiatrist Reveals How Political Correctness in Her Profession Endangers Every Student.* New York: Sentinel, 2007.

Jennifer S. Hirsch et al. — *The Secret: Love, Marriage, and HIV.* Nashville, TN: Vanderbilt University Press, 2009.

Rajasingam S. Jeyendran and Megan Hollingsworth — *Sex, Sperm, & STD's: What Every Teenage Boy Needs to Know.* Bloomington, IN: iUniverse, 2006.

Shobha S. Krishnan — *The HPV Vaccine Controversy: Sex, Cancer, God, and Politics: A Guide for Parents, Women, Men, and Teenagers.* Westport, CT: Praeger, 2008.

Laura Larsen, ed. — *Sexually Transmitted Diseases: Sourcebook.* 4th ed. Detroit, MI: Omnigraphics, 2009.

Alexandra M. Lord — *Condom Nation: The U.S. Government's Sex Education Campaign from World War I to the Internet*. Baltimore, MD: Johns Hopkins University Press, 2010.

Lisa Marr — *Sexually Transmitted Diseases: A Physician Tells You What You Need to Know*. 2nd ed. Baltimore, MD: Johns Hopkins University Press, 2007.

Elaine A. Moore with Lisa Marie Moore — *Encyclopedia of Sexually Transmitted Diseases*. Jefferson, NC: McFarland, 2008.

Timothy R. Moss and Alison J. Woodland, eds. — *Chlamydia: The Silent Disease*. Jupiter, FL: Merit Publishing, 2008.

Adina Nack — *Damaged Goods? Women Living with Incurable Sexually Transmitted Diseases*. Philadelphia, PA: Temple University Press, 2008.

John Paranscandola — *Sex, Sin, and Science: A History of Syphilis in America*. Westport, CT: Praeger, 2008.

Elizabeth Pisani — *The Wisdom of Whores: Bureaucrats, Brothels, and the Business of AIDS*. New York: W.W. Norton & Co., 2008.

John H. Stokes — *The Third Great Plague: A Discussion of Syphilis for Everyday People*. Charleston, SC: BibioBazaar, 2006.

Jessica Valenti
The Purity Myth: How America's Obsession with Virginity Is Hurting Young Women. Berkeley, CA: Seal Press, 2009.

Keith Wailoo et al., eds.
Three Shots at Prevention: The HPV Vaccine and the Politics of Medicine's Simple Solutions. Baltimore, MD: Johns Hopkins University Press, 2010.

Terri Warren
The Good News About the Bad News: Herpes, Everything You Need to Know. Oakland, CA: New Harbinger Publications, 2009.

Index